LINDA CLARK

is rapidly becoming America's number one writer on healthful living. Of the many books that she has written, many have been, and remain, best sellers. She writes a column for two health publications and is editor of a well-known health magazine. For many years she has conducted a daily radio program on the West Coast and has spoken at nutritional meetings across the country.

COLOR THERAPY

Reports state that a four-year-old child dying from an asthma attack was given an injection. The injection had no effect. Then a doctor instructed the child's mother to tie a red ribbon around the child's wrist. Four hours later, the child sat up, and by evening, was back to normal. This and other case histories illustrate the apparent healing properties of color therapy. **The Ancient Art of Color Therapy** "is a fascinating attempt to explain the lore of color . . . very impressive." —*Los Angeles Times*

Books by Linda Clark

The Ancient Art of Color Therapy
Handbook of Natural Remedies for Common Ailments

Published by POCKET BOOKS

The Ancient Art of
COLOR THERAPY

LINDA CLARK

PUBLISHED BY POCKET BOOKS NEW YORK

POCKET BOOKS, a Simon & Schuster division of
GULF & WESTERN CORPORATION
1230 Avenue of the Americas, New York, N.Y. 10020

Published by arrangement with Devin-Adair Company
Library of Congress Catalog Card Number: 74-75388

ISBN: 0-671-42133-6

First Pocket Books printing April, 1978

10   9   8   7   6   5   4

POCKET and colophon are trademarks of Simon & Schuster.

Printed in the U.S.A.

Contents

	Publisher's Preface	7
	Author's Preface	9
	A Note to the Reader	11
1.	The Beneficial Effects of Light	15
2.	Natural versus Artificial Light	33
3.	How Light and Color Work	43
4.	The Psychological Impact of Color	53
5.	Color and Physical Health	65
6.	Color and Nutrition	73
7.	Color Therapy for Eye Problems	83
8.	How to Apply Color Therapy	91
9.	Properties of Individual Colors	105
10.	Gem Therapy and Amulets	131
11.	Auras	155
12.	Breathing Color	169
	Bibliography	185

Publisher's Preface

When the Founding Fathers hammered our Constitution together, there was skepticism on the part of certain delegates. A fear that they might have created an instrument that could result in the exercise of too much power by government. Having defeated one tyranny, they feared another. Accordingly, they added ten amendments which came to be known as The Bill of Rights. Number one dealt with freedom of speech: "Congress shall make no law . . . abridging freedom of speech or of the press. . . ." There it was—and still is—spelled right out.

Unfortunately, the delegates failed to visualize bureaucratic edict which today governs us more effectively—and more tyrannically—than Congress. For forty years weak Congresses have allowed the federal bureaucracy to grow into the monster it is today. Its edicts have the force of law and all that goes with it. It takes a brave, and well-heeled, citizen to oppose it.

Color therapy—using color to influence human health—belongs in the category of fringe medicine. To some it is "way out," to others it is "pure quackery." But to those who have benefitted by

7

it, and they number in the thousands, it is a life-saver. Despite its proved record of healing over the centuries, and despite the First Amendment's clearly spelled out intentions, a federal bureau, the Food and Drug Administration, in league with the American Medical Association, has declared that unorthodox medicine (such as color therapy), not only must not be practiced, but its methods and applications may not even be written about. That is why the reader of this discussion of an ancient art must be denied the names and addresses of those individuals—doctors and lay practitioners—who have been and are achieving results, many of them spectacular, with color therapy. And that is why the author is constrained from telling the reader specifically how to use these time-tested methods. That would be construed as "practicing medicine" and she would be subject to prosecution or harassment, as others have been.

It should be clearly understood that the FDA has done some good in protecting the public from contaminated food and some dangerous drugs such as Thalidomide. For this sort of action we must be grateful.

It is when it comes to preventive medicine and to natural, drugless, methods of healing that the FDA exerts intolerant and ruthless tyranny. As a consequence, much of the information in this book amounts to circumlocution, and the reader is invited to look between the lines and to exercise his own imagination wherever possible. A little research on the general subject of color therapy will prove rewarding.

—DEVIN A. GARRITY

Author's Preface

Color therapy is centuries old. Five hundred years before the birth of Christ, Pythagoras used color for healing. Today, color therapy still makes sense, but many people refuse to believe it can affect both physical and mental health. Such people forget that, like different forms of light, heat and sound, each color has its own specific frequency or wave length which is a measurable, provable source of energy. When this form of energy is beamed on a plant, animal or person, something happens. Scientists are discovering countless effects of color, and thus are providing a logical explanation for a system of therapy long considered merely folk lore, but which is now definitely established by laboratory experiments as valid.

It is true that color therapy is not always a swift method of healing, just as proper nutrition rarely brings overnight results. These natural methods do not mask symptoms as drugs do, but have been found to help rebuild and regenerate the body. This usually (though not always) takes time. Meanwhile many people, impatient for instant results, may conclude that such remedies do not work at all. Not true! There is too much testimony to the contrary. The effect on the body may be slower, but it is also longer lasting. Using the right prescription for color (as well as the right type of nutrition) and given a fair chance, both methods can be a part of Nature's way of gradually restoring health.

Color therapy is used successfully in other countries. But until the American people demand that its use be sanctioned in the United States, it will continue to be restricted here.

This book is the result of twenty years of research; it covers the information found in nearly every major book ever written on the subject.

I hope it will open your eyes to something special which may have been missing from your life, and will encourage you to explore further into a fascinating subject that has much to offer. Color therapy has become a lost art and now seems the time to revive it.

—LINDA CLARK

A Note to the Reader

Neither the author nor publisher of this book make any claims as to the positive (or negative) effects of color on health, disease, nutrition or any other human functions. The information contained in the pages that follow represents research conducted by various investigators in many parts of the world and which, for the most part, has been taken from the books and periodicals listed in the footnotes and bibliography.

The author is a reporter, not a physician, and is not able to reply to any correspondence or questions in connection with color therapy. However, if you know of additional sources of information, or have successful experiences yourself and wish to communicate them to the author, she will be delighted to learn more about this fascinating subject. Letters should be addressed to Linda Clark, c/o The Devin-Adair Company, Old Greenwich, Conn. 06870.

The ANCIENT ART
of COLOR THERAPY

1. The Beneficial Effects of Light

I am interested in anything that can improve health naturally. For years I had heard of color therapy, but either the secrets were guarded, or the available information was so scant that it was almost impossible to get exact facts on what color could accomplish for health. I hunted for books and help from individuals the world over, searching for any and every shred of available information. I often ran into a stone wall. Many of the books had either been destroyed or were out of print; or those that still existed were published in other countries, especially England or India. I eventually found a single extant book here and there, which I borrowed. I also questioned some serious students of the art who somewhat fearfully supplied knowledge they had learned but asked that their names not be mentioned. Some were actually terrified of being found out after witnessing what had happened to their revered teachers who had spent lifetimes studying color therapy, only to be persecuted for teaching or practicing it. Books and equipment had been destroyed in certain instances and there was little information left except via word of mouth. No wonder it took me so long to get the information that appears here!

There seems to be a widespread attempt to stamp out knowledge of certain natural health practices, and to intimidate anyone using them in competition with orthodox treatment. This particularly applies to physiological health; psychological health appears to be less in jeopardy. If you think this assault on color therapy to be far-fetched, consider the present similar attempt to deprive the public of freedom of choice in the case of natural, or "organic," foods and vitamin/mineral supplements. The excuse given for such assaults on health freedom is that the action is for "your protection." This is a myth. Why outlaw *safe* therapies such as nutrition and color therapy and allow *dangerous* drugs to be sold with no strings attached? So it seemed time to take the cover off color therapy in order that you might see what it can do and, if you wish, use it in your own home.

Skeptics may say that the effects of color are "all in the mind," but studies with plants and animals prove otherwise. Reports from people are also impressive. For example, one woman told me, after studying the method with her teacher (an M.D., now elderly and retired, whose whereabouts she refuses to disclose for his safety), that by inserting lenses of certain colors in special eyeglass frames for a short time each day, she was able to reduce the amount of insulin necessary to control her diabetes.

Another woman, too overstimulated to take a much needed nap during the daytime, fell into a restful sleep for two-and-a-half hours after being exposed to blue light.

A physician, trained in color therapy in Europe,

reports that beaming blue light on the body area following an injection of a nutritional substance relaxed the area and accelerated the body's pick-up of the substance.

These are only a few of countless reports of successful color therapy.

In case you contend that these people who report their own success with color for health are merely deluded, let me assure you that they are not. The first woman, a good friend, is an intelligent owner of an automotive-parts factory. The success of this factory is undeniably due to her stability and good judgment. The second woman is my daughter, who was told of the blue light for relaxation and sleep by her doctor who believes in color therapy, though, as a rule, he dares not practice it. The third, the physician, recently left the United States so that he can practice as he wishes elsewhere.

To help you understand why and how color works, we must first consider the beneficial effects of light. For instance, by learning what sunlight, the total source of all colors, can accomplish, it is easier to understand why and how specific, separate colors may be especially effective.

To show you the power of healing from light and color, I am going to quote verbatim from the research findings of respected physicians and scientists who have used such therapy successfully in the past before it became forbidden.

To start with, here is an abstract of a paper presented by Kate W. Baldwin, M.D., F.A.C.S., at the clinical meeting of the Section on Eye, Ear, Nose and Throat Diseases of the Medical Society of the State of Pennsylvania, October 12, 1926, as printed in *The Atlantic Medical Journal* (April, 1927):

For centuries, scientists have devoted untiring efforts to discover means for the relief or cure of human ills and restoration of the normal functions. Yet in neglected light and color there is a potency far beyond that of drugs and serums.

In order that the whole body may function perfectly, each organ must be a hundred per cent perfect. When the spleen, the liver, or any other organ falls below normal, it simply means that the body laboratories have not provided the required materials with which to work, either because they are not functioning, as a result of some disorder of the internal mechanism, or because they have not been provided with the necessary materials. Before the body can appropriate the required elements, they must be separated from the waste matter. Each element gives off a characteristic color wave. The prevailing color wave of hydrogen is red, and that of oxygen is blue, and each element in turn gives off its own special color wave. Sunlight, as it is received by the body, is split into the prismatic colors and their combinations, as white light is split by passage through a prism. Everything on the red side of the spectrum is more or less stimulating, while the blue is sedative. There are many shades of each color, and each is produced by a little different wave length. Just as sound waves are tuned to each other and produce harmony or discords, so color waves may be tuned, and only so can they be depended on always to produce the same results. . . . Color is the simplest and most accurate therapeutic measure yet developed.

For about six years I have given close attention to the action of colors in restoring the body functions, and I am perfectly honest in saying that, after nearly thirty-seven years of active hospital and private practice in medicine and surgery, I can produce quicker and more accurate results with colors than with any or all other methods combined—and with less strain on the patient. In many cases, the functions have been restored after the classical remedies have failed. Of course, surgery is necessary in some cases, but results will be quicker and better if color is used before and after operation. Sprains, bruises and traumata of all sorts respond to color as to no other treatment. Septic conditions yield, regardless of the specific organism. Cardiac lesions, asthma, hay fever, pneumonia, inflammatory conditions of the eyes, corneal ulcers, glaucoma, and cataracts are relieved by the treatment.

The treatment of carbuncles with color is easy compared to the classical methods. One woman with a carbuncle involving the back of the neck from mastoid to mastoid, and from occipital ridge to the first dorsal vertebra, came under color therapy after ten days of the very best of attention. From the first day of color application, no opiates, not even sedatives, were required. This patient was saved much suffering, and she has little scar.

The use of color in the treatment of burns is well worth investigation by every member of the profession. In such cases the burning sensation caused by the destructive forces may be counteracted in from twenty to thirty minutes, and it does not return. True burns are caused by the destructive action of the red side of the spectrum, hydrogen predominating. Apply oxygen by the use of the blue side of the spectrum, and much will be done to relieve the nervous strain, the healing processes are rapid, and the resulting tissues soft and flexible.

In a very extensive burn in a child of eight years of age there was almost complete suppression of urine for more than 48 hours, with a temperature of 105 to 106 degrees. Fluids were forced to no effect, and a more hopeless case was seldom seen. Scarlet was applied just over the kidneys at a distance of eighteen inches for twenty minutes, all other areas being covered. Two hours after, the child voided eight ounces of urine.

In some unusual and extreme cases that had not responded to other treatment, normal functioning has been restored by color therapy. At present, therefore, I do not feel justified in refusing any case without a trial. Even in cases where death is inevitable, much comfort may be secured.

There is no question that light and color are important therapeutic media, and that their adoption will be of advantage to both the profession and the people.

THE SUN AND HEALTH

Edward Podolsky, M.D., in pointing out that the sun is the source of all life on earth, and also the source of light and heat—the two types of energy required by all living things—reminds us:

When Newton analyzed a beam of sunlight by means of a triangular piece of glass (a prism) he found that the beam consisted of many colors. For this reason it has been held that black is the absence of color, while white is a combination of all colors. *Sunlight is a combination of all colors of the spectrum, visible and invisible.*

From very early times, Dr. Podolsky adds, it has been known that the sun is a source of health; perhaps a subconscious recognition of this fact was the actuating factor of the sun worship of primitive religions. Sun-bathing dates back to antiquity. The love of basking in the sun seems to be inherent in all living creatures.

Today, more than ever before, sunlight is recognized as a powerful factor in building and maintaining health. In many cases in which other remedial measures have failed, sunlight has been found to exert a favorable influence.

William Benham Snow, M.D., explains why: "The effect of light and heat radiations upon metabolism is to quicken the functional activities of the cells thus stimulated, promoting elimination through sweat glands, and inducing an increased influx of blood . . . thereby favoring local nutrition and elimination. . . . These effects, in a general way, indicate the therapeutic employment of light . . . from a natural source (the sun), and artificial sources (the use of lamps, filters, etc)."

We know that most plants kept out of sunlight become pale and spindly. Sun-starved people also exhibit pallor. I witnessed this fact during a vacation one summer on Nantucket Island, Massachusetts. Each day the ferry arrived bringing a load of passengers, many of them New York City and Boston office workers. As these people left the boat, they appeared pale and pasty-faced from many months of sunlight starvation. Two weeks later when they reboarded the boat after their vacation was over, they were rosy, tanned and healthy-looking from exposure to the sun at the beaches. So every day a load of pale people arrived, and another load of healthy, transformed pale-faces boarded the boat to return to their city homes and offices. William J. Fielding, another researcher, writes:

On the surface, it may seem rather farfetched to allude to "sunlight starvation" as a condition that periodically undermines the health and well-being of countless numbers of people in the Northern temperate zone. Notwithstanding occasional cloudy and stormy weather, there would seem to be a goodly number of bright and clear days, to which the great majority of our people have fairly free access.

However, from November to May, there is so great

a reduction in the short-ray radiations that reach the earth in the Northern latitudes that a very considerable proportion of the general population of these parts may truly be said to suffer from "sunlight starvation."

This reminds me of a woman, whom I had not seen, who was being described to me by a friend.

"Does she look healthy?" I asked.

My friend hesitated, and then said, "Well, not really; she doesn't look as if she spent much time outdoors."

After moving to California, I was curious about why so many Californians, particularly women, looked more healthy and vital than eastern women. I soon learned that because of the climate they can spend more time out-of-doors the year round. But their husbands who spend so much time in their offices do not look as healthy. William J. Fielding adds:

California, which apparently gets more effective sunlight than any other portion of this country, has the most luxurious flowers, the best fruits and the largest trees. The draft board statistics showed that the best developed men came from the Pacific Coast region, where the pure sunshine, the great open spaces and more natural mode of life, combined to produce the finest specimens of physical manhood.

ANEMIA FROM LIGHT DEFICIENCY

In their book, *Light and Health*, Luckiesh and Pacini write:

The great majority of observers have furnished abundant evidence that there is a decrease in the red-cell count . . . when the organism is placed in darkness.

There have been numerous investigations on the effect of sunlight and other radiations on the number of red blood cells present in the blood. . . . Enough observers have obtained sufficiently convincing results to make one believe that there is a decrease in the red-cell count and in the hemoglobin percentage in the dark, and an increase in the light. These changes are not permanent, the blood later tending to right itself in most instances.

It was noted in the case of a large number of men in government employ who were shifted to night work that a retreat from sunlight . . . was followed by a lowering of the number of red blood cells and the quantity of hemoglobin in the blood, and that the hemoglobin suffers a greater decrease in amount than do the red cells in number. While several factors might easily account for these changes, the induced anemia appeared to be ascribed to a light deficiency more than any other cause. . . .

OTHER AILMENTS FROM SUN STARVATION

Researcher William Fielding notes:

As the intensity of sunlight wanes in November and remains feeble until May, there comes a season of typical sunlight starvation. Scores of curious effects are coincident with this period of abiotic light. The most virile infections such as typhoid and influenza rage at this time. Respiratory diseases are at their height. And it is not impossible that the organisms responsible for these dreaded diseases find the body more anemic at this time than at any other, and therefore more susceptible to infection.

Dr. Podolsky also cites health benefits from sunlight:

The influence of the sun's combined colors on general

health is remarkable. Pain, fever and chills disappear readily, and the condition of the blood is often improved. Both hemoglobin and the red cells increase and the general composition of the blood is enriched. As a result, anemic, chlorotic and scrofulous patients have been found to derive immeasurable benefit from sun-baths. Sunlight exercises a powerful action on the nourishment of all living animals. When the rays penetrate the depths of the body they increase the metabolism in all the tissues. This action is also bactericidal and pain relieving.

Sinus infections and ulcers react markedly to sunlight; the profuse discharge that occurs at first is followed by sloughing, the formation of healthy tissue, and a gradual drying and healing of the sinus infection or ulcer. Sunlight reduces the volume of pus abscesses and frequently causes complete absorption. The rays of the sun cause a similar absorption of fluids in the joints, abdominal and lung cavities. This is especially noticeable in peritonitis.

Sunlight also stimulates the heart and other vital organs. It produces an increase in the oxidation of protein, which in turn causes a rise of temperature. Perspiration is increased, causing an extra amount of poisonous material to be eliminated. Sometimes the increase in perspiration is from 2¼ ounces an hour, which is the normal amount, to as much as 2 to 3 pounds an hour. Sunlight stimulates the nervous system, improving the appetite and mental attitude and inducing better sleep.

How Sunlight Is Administered

Dr. Podolsky explains:

In 1903 Dr. A. Rollier opened at Leysin (French Switzerland) his world-famous clinic for the systematized sun treatment of surgical tuberculosis.

Rollier's method of treatment begins by exposing the patient's body to the rays of the sun for periods of from five to ten minutes. Usually the new patient's feet are exposed for five minutes twice or three times the first day, for ten minutes the second day, and so on. The legs are exposed for five minutes twice or three times the second day, ten the third day, etc. until in about two weeks the entire body is exposed for from three to six hours daily. The prescription of sun exposure for each patient is an individual calculation, and many factors, such as altitude, humidity, the angle at which the principal ray strikes the patient, as well as the sensitiveness and age of the patient have all to be taken into consideration.

Rollier has achieved such success in the treatment of some tubercular conditions of the extremities that limbs which other surgeons had advised amputating were restored for use. The proportion of cures effected under Rollier's treatment ranges upward of ninety per cent of the cases he receives, and this is all the more remarkable when we consider that the great majority of them are in advanced stages, coming to him as a last resort after having tried unsuccessfully various other forms of treatment. They come to him from all parts of the world.

Light, Dr. Rollier declares, is the best masseur. At any rate, we find that the stimulating light, playing upon the nude skin in the dry, cool air, induces and maintains that condition of tone in the muscles which, without moving any joints, is yet a form of muscular activity essential for the production of bodily heat and for the proper posture of the bodily parts.

Dr. Podolsky concludes:

Indeed, the sun's rays possess so wide a range of usefulness that it is interesting to recall that Dr. O. Bernard found that a reopened abdominal wall, which would not heal under ordinary treatment, almost immediately assumed a better aspect following several hours' exposure to the sun, and closed quite rapidly thereafter.

Luckiesh and Pacini suggest an explanation for such healings: "It was shown many years ago that sunlight retards the growth of bacteria. The effect was proved not due to heat; *the killing of the bacteria is more pronounced as the wave length of the effective light becomes shorter.*" (Emphasis added.)

Edwin D. Babbitt, M.D., author of a very rare book, *The Principles of Light and Color*, published in 1878 (the original version is long out of print), devoted much of his medical practice to the use of color therapy on his patients. He stated:

While many conditions of disease may be improved by exposure to one or more colors, the combined colors, as in white light, are the ones which man and nature must generally depend upon, and which most of all they require. . . . By exposing any portion of the body to the sun, *not to an undue extent*, the skin becomes somewhat darker, clearer and more rosy than the waxy bleached whiteness of indoor faces . . . put the pale, withering plant or human being into the sun, and if not too far gone, each will recover health and spirit.

SOME EFFECTS OF SUN STARVATION

According to Dr. Babbitt:

Foureault affirms that where there is want of light are seen the stunted forms and general deterioration of the human race. In Chimay, Belgium, 3,000 workers were engaged partly as coal miners, partly as field laborers. The field laborers were robust and readily supplied their proper number of recruits to the army; among the miners it was in most years impossible to find a man who was eligible due to some body deformity or arrest of physical development.

Forbes Winslow, in his book, *Light, Its Influence on Life and Health,* states that those who live and work where there is a minimum of natural light suffer seriously in body and mental health. Even on the shady side of deep valleys, cretinism has been observed. Animals that live underground, and people who rarely see natural light, suffer from visual deterioration as well as physical illnesses. Animals that live underground continuously may actually lose their vision. A male photographer who spent much time in the dark room nearly became blind until he was regularly re-exposed to the sun, as attested to by Dr. John Ott, and described in the next chapter.

Florence Nightingale, realizing the importance of natural sunlight on health, insisted upon allowing sunlight in the sick room. Yet I know of at least one public school in the United States—and there are undoubtedly others—with windows of *black glass* purposely to block out natural sunlight in the classrooms. (The artificial fluorescent lights are not an acceptable substitute, as we shall see.) I shudder at the eventual effects on the health of the poor children who attend such schools!

Dr. Babbitt cited the case of a woman, residing in Paris, who had suffered from an enormous complication of diseases which had baffled the skill of her medical advisers. They decided that her case was almost hopeless. Finally, an eminent surgeon suggested that she be taken out of the dark room in which she lived and moved to a lighter, brighter area where she could expose herself to sunlight as much as possible. Her improvement was rapid and she recovered completely.

Audrey Kargere tells of a woman, who was both feeble and subject to colds, who became healthier and practically immune to colds after taking sunbaths on her skin. So the power of the sun can recharge; but the healing power of the sun can also be derived from the colors, used separately for separate conditions. Dr. Kargere writes:

All white light is composed of all colors. Pure sunlight vitalizes the general system, especially the skin, and in warm seasons is particularly stimulating and healing. Tumors and colds and other diseases have been reversed by sunlight used in moderation. Sunlight combines both thermal (warm) and electrical rays (color frequencies), and covers every variety of power by exposing any part of the body to the sun for a reasonable length of time . . . to avoid sunstroke, wear a well-ventilated hat with a blue lining.

Pliny stated that the secret of Rome's becoming the mightiest of nations for six hundred years, was that the Romans maintained solaria on the roofs of their houses where they took frequent sun-and-air baths.

EFFECTS OF OVEREXPOSURE TO SUNLIGHT

It is unwise to go to the opposite extreme and become overexposed to sunlight. As beneficial, and as necessary as sunlight is for health and well-being, overexposure can be detrimental, even dangerous. Those who are regularly overexposed, such as fishermen and desert natives, develop leathery, weather-beaten, prematurely aged and wrinkled skins, which cannot be reversed. Skin cancer and sunstroke can also occur in some people overexposed to the sun. As people are learning of these hazards, sun hats are coming back into use. Those who take their sun tanning seriously should acquire a tan gradually, preferably before 10:00 A.M. and after 3:00 P.M. when some of the sun's rays are less intense.

There is no point in burning yourself to a crisp. Pigmentation is nature's protection against too bright sunlight. There has long been a fad to acquire a suntan color ranging from light copper to deep chocolate, but medical and beauty experts now consider tanning to a light biscuit shade far safer. Those who swim, play golf, work in their gardens, or walk daily may get enough sun on their arms, legs, and even on face and neck under a hat, to supply their average sun needs. Luckiesh and Pacini warn:

Overexposure to intense radiation can be harmful; yet to be deprived of radiant energy is no less harmful to the body. A large number of curious bone diseases apparently may be traced back to the advent of wearing clothes in the dawn of civilization. For example, rickets, a disease in which the bones soften, is unknown in light-loving animals. It is also one of a number of diseases which, in the temperate climates, are classed under the name of "sunlight starvation" which continues from November to May, the seasons when sunlight is at its lowest ebb on our earth. [The Northern Hemisphere. Smog adds to the effect.]

Exposure of the body to ultraviolet radiation increases metabolic activity . . . promotes and enhances cellular regeneration of the part receiving the radiation. However, if the exposure is overdone, or if radiation of very short wave lengths is used instead, the superficial layers of cytoplasm are quickly coagulated and thus furnish a sclerotic barrier to the generalized metabolic responses just mentioned. Here again, intelligent discrimination is required. In other words, use moderation.

Ultraviolet light is beneficial under the right conditions. Without it, sun-loving plants will not grow properly, and health benefits may be restricted. It appears, however, that no hard and fast rule can be made as to how much ultraviolet is safe. The expert on light, Dr. John N. Ott, says:

There is no simple answer as to just how long a person may be safely exposed to ultraviolet rays. It depends upon the intensity of sunlight, the time of day, season of the year and the geographical location. A person in northern Canada would receive on an early winter morning a very small fraction of ultraviolet compared to the amount received near the equator on a summer day at noon. The amount of smog in various areas can also filter out some of the rays.

There are also differences in the sensitivity or resistance to ultraviolet in different people, especially in fair, light-skinned individuals compared to those with a darker skin. Another variable to consider is whether a person has built up any resistance to sunlight over a period of time by regular exposure to sun, or has been working in an office all year, with little or no exposure at all.

Although natural vegetable oil, or cocoa butter, are safe to use on an over-dry skin, John Ott himself prefers not to use a suntan lotion for two reasons: it may block the admission of the ultraviolet rays through the skin, or may interfere with nature's alarm system which lets us know by redden-

ing and burning that you are getting too much
ultraviolet.

Dr. Podolsky concludes: "As an indication of
proper treatment, it may be set down as a general
rule that a sun-bath should be limited to produce
in everyone the sensation of comfort and well-
being, followed by the sensation of increased
strength."

2. Natural versus Artificial Light

Perhaps you have seen the beautiful time-lapse films of flowers and plants actually growing before your eyes. Dr. John N. Ott is one of the top photographers responsible for these history-making films, originally made for Walt Disney Studios. His motion pictures have telescoped time so that the graceful development and opening of a flower, which usually takes weeks, could be shown in all its awe-inspiring detail within a few minutes. However, originally this type of photography presented some serious problems which have since turned out to be an invaluable lesson for mankind.

In order to catch the different stages of growth of plants or blossoms, it was necessary to wait for a little growth to take place between pictures—perhaps a few minutes or a few hours, depending on the species. Because of the cold climate in which Dr. Ott lived, it was also necessary at times to move a plant from out-of-doors, where it received natural sunlight, into a greenhouse which was artificially lighted by fluorescent bulbs. This often caused trouble.

Under so-called "cool-white" fluorescent lights, which are actually slightly pinkish, a plant's male flowers thrived, but the female buds turned brown and dropped off. On the other hand, "daylight white" bulbs, which give off a bluish light, caused female blossoms to thrive, while the male blossoms withered and died—often right in the middle of a photographic sequence. This was most frustrating.

Even plants exposed to ordinary window glass reacted differently to indoor sunshine than to outdoor sunshine. The reasons: most ordinary glass prevents some ninety-nine percent of the admission of ultraviolet radiation. This reminded Dr. Ott of the old-time practice of removing glass sash from cold frames during the daytime to expose young seedlings to direct natural sunlight. So he conceived the idea of making a greenhouse of the type of plastic that admits ninety-five percent of the ultraviolet rays. Apples previously grown behind glass had refused to ripen, but when the glass was replaced with the ultraviolet-admitting plastic, the apples began to show red in two days. Tomatoes which became infected with a virus in a glass greenhouse recovered and put forth healthy new growth.

Growth of plants would continue under ordinary light bulbs, but blossoms often refused to set as readily as under natural sunlight. However, the fluorescent bulbs appeared to be the real troublemakers.

Dr. Ott later found that animals subjected to fluorescent lighting also reacted in a manner similar to plants. Chinchillas raised outdoors under natural light produced almost an even number of male and female offspring. Under pinkish fluorescent lights, the litters, like the plants raised under the same lights, were almost all male; under bluish light they were almost all female. When both pink and white fluorescent lights were turned on fourteen hours a day, tropical fish stopped producing. Fish exposed to the bluish fluorescent light still did not produce, while those under pink light did, but twenty percent of their offspring were sexual freaks.

Tails of both male and female mice become spotted after only twelve hours of daily exposure to cool-white or daylight-white fluorescent light and within three months become raw. Tail-spotting occurred even sooner under gold fluorescent lighting and was still more rapid under pink fluorescent light. Complete necrosis (death or loss of tissue) of the tail was evident in mice exposed to pink fluorescent light for six months, as proved by before-and-after photographs. Tail deterioration subsided when the mice were transferred to a cage illuminated by natural sunlight. Dr. Ott adds:

Since the beginning of time, life on this earth has evolved under natural sunlight. . . . The benefits of sunlight on the skin, synthesizing vitamin D, are well known. However, we are just beginning to find that light, *entering the eyes*, in addition to vision, stimulates activity in both the pituitary and pineal glands and possibly other areas in the mid-brain and hypothalamia regions. These control the endocrine system and the production of hormones. Thus, light energy exerts an influence on the (human) body chemistry, as it does . . . on plants.

Recent experimental studies have indicated that abnormal growth responses develop when any part of the natural sunlight spectral energy is blocked from entering the eyes.*

---

* John N. Ott: "Responses of Psychological and Physiological Functions to Environmental Light," *Journal of Learning Disabilities,* June 1969

In his book, *My Ivory Cellar*, Dr. Ott writes:

The poultry industry knows that light received through the chickens' eyes stimulates the pituitary gland and increases egg production. This may be an important clue. The pituitary gland is the master balance wheel of the entire glandular system, not only in chickens but in other animals and humans as well. If this is so, and the entire glandular system can be affected, or glandular actions modified by light received through the eye, the resulting consequences and possibilities of what this might mean are utterly fantastic.

Luckiesh and Pacini, who wrote earlier, believe this concept may be a factor in rejuvenation. They write:

Possibly all the glands of internal secretion are involved in the drama of old age, since the condition is definitely associated with symptoms which can be traced to the failure of several glands . . . all of the glands of internal secretion atrophy and become exhausted as old age advances. . . . The glands dominantly affected by old age include the thyroid, pituitary and adrenals which, together with the sex glands, are most influenced by light and ultraviolet radiation. The solution to the problem of rejuvenation may possibly lie hidden in the many secrets of radiation. . . .

Those who have had experience with this practice can recite many remarkable transformations. The general appearance becomes more youthful. Fat persons have reduced considerably in weight and thin persons have gained, both reactions perhaps being expression of internal gland equilibrium. . . .

When the blood of workmen was tested for adrenal activity, a marked lessening of adrenal activity was observed during the period of the year which corresponded with diminished muscular strength. Since the adrenal glands are profoundly influenced by light, especially by ultraviolet radiation, naturally it seemed logical to infer that the winter's diminishing ultraviolet intensity lessened not only adrenal stimulation, but also caused corresponding increase of fatigue which brought with it muscle weakness and decreased effort accomplishment. . . . To test this hypothesis . . . ultraviolet radiation was furnished workmen under medical supervision. Work production was no longer seriously impaired; blood sugar remained more nearly normal throughout the season, and the test for adrenal insufficiency showed a barely perceptible lag, proving that the failing light quality of winter plays an important part in muscular stamina which reflects immediately in inefficient work production. Light, unquestionably, has much to do with muscle tone and vigor.

Winter is not the only light-limiting factor, however. Dr. Ott reminds us that the majority of people spend approximately ninety percent of their time behind glass—walls and windows of closed buildings, offices, homes, buses and cars. They also wear eyeglasses and sunglasses. All of these prevent natural light from being admitted through the eyes to the glandular system. What is the result? Although few studies on people have been conducted on the subject, Dr. Ott accidentally made a discovery in connection with his own health.

He had long been crippled with arthritis, could walk only with a cane, and doctors recommended the use of walking braces. Hoping Florida sunshine would help him, he spent hours on the beach there, soaking up the sun, being careful to wear sunglasses to protect his eyes from the bright sunlight. Yet he noticed no change in his arthritis until, one day, he broke his sunglasses. In the next few days he experienced dramatic improvement. He found that his arthritis improved when he spent long daylight hours outdoors *without his glasses*. He was finally able to discard his collection of canes. His vision also improved, he says, and sore throats and colds became less frequent. His friends who followed suit reported success with various disorders, ranging from bleeding gums to bursitis. Dr. Ott is convinced that by spending so much time behind ordinary window glass, eyeglasses, even car windshields, we are actually inviting poor health!

His next step was to build a house with plastic window panes which, as in the greenhouse, admit the rays of natural sunlight. He says:

If the theory of the importance of the full spectrum of sunlight energy proves to be true, it will necessitate some changes in our present way of living. It will mean using certain types of plastic or glass which will permit the transmission of ultraviolet and other wave lengths of light energy (for houses, offices, windshields and spectacles) . . . it will also mean that artificial lights will have to be developed that more closely give off the same distribution of energy as natural sunlight.

Dr. Ott tells of the experience of an associate photographer who had spent many hours under fluorescent lights. He was a diabetic and had become nearly blind, so that he had been scarcely able to distinguish day from night. For four years he had also been troubled with hemorrhaging eye blood vessels. At Dr. Ott's suggestion, he began to spend more time outdoors. After six months of exposure to natural daylight at every possible minute, he began to see the outline of the sidewalk and his eye blood vessels ceased to burst.

The manager of a radio station, after hearing Dr. Ott lecture, suddenly realized the disturbance fluorescents had caused in his radio station. To make the light appear more attractive in the studios, pink fluorescent tubes had been installed. Within two months, staff members became quarrelsome with each other, and the management and two men threatened to resign. Finally, one announcer said: "If those blankety blank lights aren't removed, I am going to go out of my mind."

The pink tubes were removed that very day and natural tubes were substituted. Within a week, as if by a miracle, tempers ceased to flare, congeniality returned, the resignations were withdrawn, and work improved generally.

Thus, the time-lapse photography initiated by John Ott is teaching us important concepts which can affect not only plants, but animals and people. This explains why, in the school I mentioned earlier where the window glass is black, shutting out all natural light, and where the lighting is fluorescent only, problems are bound to occur sooner or later. The teachers are already noticing it, and are concerned about increasing emotional upsets and other disturbing symptoms evident among the children, although this school is comparatively new.

The effect of the absence of natural light, both upon the skin and through the eyes is not mere guess work. To date Dr. Ott has spent more than forty years of research on the subject of lighting and its effect upon health. He is now Chairman and Executive Director of the Environmental Health and Light Research Institute in Sarasota, Florida. His work is being noted with respect internationally. His most recent book is called *Health and Light.* It was published in 1973 and is highly recommended for the general reader. (See Bibliography.)

Meanwhile, Dr. Ott's discoveries have led to practical reforms. There is now available a full spectrum transmitting lens for contact lenses, produced by Obrig Laboratories in Sarasota, Florida. There is another optical company making lenses for spectacles which admit the full-light spectrum, including ultraviolet. These lenses (they are plastic) are available in clear, for regular spectacles, or in gray for sunglasses. Because of Dr. Ott's own experiences with ordinary sunglasses, he frowns on their use because they admit the spectrum of light *unevenly,* and eliminate ultraviolet *entirely.* After all, according to Ott's research, much of the benefit of the ultraviolet light is due to its penetration through the eyes. The new type of gray sunglasses, made to Dr. Ott's specifications, admit the whole spectrum evenly and include the ultraviolet, which is of a safe intensity.

These spectacles or sunglasses are available through opticians, optometrists and ophthalmologists who, in turn, can order them for you at your request from Armorlite Lens Co., P.O. Box 138, Burbank, California, 91505. This company services the optical professions *only,* on a wholesale basis, so no one but your optical adviser can order them for your special lens prescription. The price varies very little from regular glasses. In order to avoid being trapped into buying the ordinary gray sunglasses (which are not correctly made and will not provide the protection you are seeking), you can get a small card which certifies that your sunglass lens is made by Armorlite.

As for safe incandescent tubes to fit into home,

office or school regular fluorescent fixtures, Dr.
Ott has developed a tube called *Vita-lite* which
duplicates natural light. I have these in my own
home and they are truly restful to the eyes. You
can write for information to Specto-lite, 1621
Bluejay Drive, Holiday, Florida, 33589. This company markets these safe, natural light tubes anywhere in the country. They can also provide information on the sources of the sheet plastic for
windows or greenhouses which also admit the full
natural spectrum of sunlight.

Many people ask what sunlamps are a safe substitute for natural sunlight on hazy or winter days.
Dr. Ott says that he prefers the *Vita-lite*. His explanation is that most sunlamps emit a high intensity, shortwave-length ultraviolet, which is both
too powerful and too potentially dangerous, since
it is capable of causing serious burns. Because it
can also harm the eyes, it is necessary to wear
goggles, and exposure should be limited to a very
short time. *Vita-lite,* on the other hand, is a low
intensity, near-ultraviolet light in incandescent
form, designed to come as close as possible to the
full outdoor, natural sunlight. You can, according
to Dr. Ott, stay under this natural light all day
long without goggles and without harm. After all,
as he explains, life on earth has evolved under this
type of balanced, natural ultraviolet light.

Exposure to other incandescent lights (such as
the ordinary bulbs in your lamps), though not as
effective as the full natural spectrum of the *Vita-
lite,* has been found to be not only safe, but effective. One fascinating study illustrates this: Two
Boston doctors, John Rock and Edmond Dewan,
treated twenty-five women some time ago for irregular menstrual cycles. The doctors asked the

patients to keep their bedroom lights burning throughout the night on the fourteenth, fifteenth and sixteenth day of their monthly cycle (the first day of menstruation was counted as day one of the cycle). It worked! All but two of the twenty-five women became more regular. A skeptical woman medic reporter decided to try the system for herself. She had suffered from irregular periods all her life. To her astonishment the light therapy method kept her cycle regular and dependable. If she missed the therapy once or twice, there was no problem. But when she omitted it continuously for three months, her irregularity returned.*

At the time this study took place (which apparently was before Dr. Ott's research on the effect of light through the eyes reaching various glands was known), no one seemed quite sure why the light used in this way produced such surprising results. Now it is possible to assume that the light shining through the closed eyelids entered the body and stimulated the activity of the sex glands.

So we cannot underestimate the effect of light, even if artificial, particularly when it is the right type of light used at the right time and in the right amount. As we begin to study colors, all of which are components of sunlight, it is necessary to sound some further warnings in a few instances. You should know *why* color works in physiological conditions, but you should know also which type of colors to avoid or handle with care. You must be intelligent in your choices of the energy which is coupled with color.

3. How Light and Color Work

Webster defines color as "the sensation resulting from stimulation of the retina of the eye by light waves of certain lengths."

In 1666, Sir Isaac Newton, who formulated the law of gravity, developed the first valuable theory of color. By admitting sunlight through a prism, he established the presence of seven basic colors in the spectrum which he named red, orange, yellow, green, blue, indigo, and violet. These colors are still used today for the spectrum. As early as the fifteenth century, Leonardo Da Vinci had suggested four primary colors: red, blue, green and yellow. And as late as 1914, Wilhelm Ostwald "rediscovered" the primary colors, but eliminated green as being a product of blue and yellow.

The light which Newton separated into seven distinct colors, each with its own wave length, is called a spectrum. Nature's most beautiful examples of the spectrum include the rainbow and the polar lights, aurora borealis and aurora australis. In painting with pigments, the three primary colors, red, blue and yellow, are mixed to produce the various secondary colors: green, orange, purple, etc.

All light is visible radiant energy and travels through space in forms of waves. It travels 186,000 miles per second in wave lengths that vary in size and energy. As it travels, it also vibrates. Below thirty-two impulses per second vibration, this radiant energy is inaudible as well as invisible. The wave lengths of the electromagnetic spectrum range from waves less than a thousandth of a millimeter in length to some that are hundreds of miles long.

Colors, light, and heat are thus related to wave lengths. These waves vary in length and the individual variations are the basis of each color. When the wave lengths are ultra short they become invisible, but color may still exist, even if it is not seen by the human eye.

Unlike sound waves or ocean waves, light waves seem to need no material medium. They can travel through empty space.

The colors of the spectrum are classified by physicists according to their wave length. One unit of measurement is called an angstrom unit (abbreviated A.U.), which equals one hundred-millionth of a centimeter, or 10^{-8} cm. All measurements given are approximate only, since there is no standard scale yet developed for establishing relative color wave lengths. For this reason authorities are in close, but not exact, agreement on these measurements. The following list shows the approximate range of wave lengths of colors in angstrom units:

Red	6000-6700 A.U.
Orange	5900-6000 A.U.
Yellow	5800-5900 A.U.

Green	5000-5500 A.U.
Blue	4700-5000 A.U.
Violet	4300-4600 A.U.

The National Bureau of Standards in Washington, D.C. has developed an Inter-Society Color Council to "define" and provide an acceptable standard of names for 267 of the almost unlimited variety of hues contained within the visible spectrum. Anyone interested in pursuing the study of color itself can write the National Bureau of Standards for their Circular Number 553 called *The ISCC-NBS Method of Designating Colors and a Dictionary of Color Names*. A color chart known as *ISCC-NBS Centroid Color Chart, NBS Standard Sample Number 2106* is also available from the same source.

The Pittsburgh Plate Glass Company states in its booklet *Color Dynamics for the Home:* "Since the types of rays in the electromagnetic spectrum possess great energy and perform definite functions, it is factual that light rays, which are part of this spectrum, *possess usable energy* [emphasis mine]. The waves of the electromagnetic spectrum serve an almost limitless number of uses— radio, television, infrared photography, ultraviolet lamps, etc."

Some of these electromagnetic energy sources are helpful; others are potentially dangerous and must be handled with discretion. Here is a brief summary of the various types and uses of electromagnetic radiations:

NAME	SOURCE	WHAT THEY DO
Cosmic Rays	Shortest Waves	Ionize Gases. Bombard Earth from Outer Space
Gamma Rays	Given off by Radium and other Radioactive Substances	Used in Cancer Treatment

NAME	SOURCE	WHAT THEY DO
X-rays	X-ray Tube	Take Pictures of Broken Bones. Detect Flaws in Machinery
Ultraviolet	Sun and Electric Arc	Take Pictures. Cause Tan. Destroy Molds and Bacteria
Visible Light	Sun and other stars. Incandescent Lamps	Make Vision Possible
Infrared (short)	Radiated from Hot Objects	Photography: Penetrate Haze; Take Pictures in Total Darkness
Infrared (long)	Heat Radiated from Hot Objects	The Heat Felt from Warmth, Cooking, etc.
Electricity	Electric Sparks and Arcs	Formerly Used in Wireless
Radio	High frequency Oscillating Circuit	Transmits Sounds
Television	Very High Frequency	Transmits Sound and Pictures
Very Long Waves	Alternating Current	Generates Light, Heat and Power

(From: *New Worlds Beyond the Atom* by Langston Day and George De La Warr, The Devin-Adair Co., Old Greenwich, Conn. 1959)

Radiations, however, do not end here. Colors radiate energy. Sound radiates energy. Even people, plants and animals radiate energy. In fact, scientists have now established that *everything in nature radiates energy.* Most emanations from bodies —animal, vegetable or mineral—are invisible to the naked eye of the average person. Some radiations, however, such as those from phosphorescent rocks and the light from glowworms or fireflies are visible. For radiations that cannot be detected by the average naked eye (although a few people *do* seem to have this radar-type vision), new electronic instruments are becoming available. One instrument, known as the thermograph, measures the infrared emanations from the human body. It scans large body areas and also registers intensities of radiations in half tones on photographic film.

Although these latter are at present recorded only in various shades of gray, they may eventually appear in color. As someone has said, "Even body heat comes in color."

Science is also beginning to learn how color can influence life. Numerous investigators have placed various plants under different color filters and have recorded variations in the rate and in the amount of growth . . . The long-wave region of the visible spectrum appears to accelerate growth, and the short-wave region appears to retard it. Dr. R. B. Withrow, a researcher, found that in long-day plants, such as stock, plants grew tallest when exposed to orange-red light. They grew next tallest in red light. The same species did not grow tall, nor did they flower at all under yellow, green or blue light, though they did produce somewhat vigorous foliage. Neither did they flower under infrared, only one step away from the visible red and red-orange in the spectrum. With such short-day plants as cosmos and salvia, red light interfered with flowering. John Ott discovered that exposure to red interrupted growth in morning glories; whereas the blue filters encouraged it.

Dr. Ott's microscopic time-lapse photographs actually showed the streaming of the protoplasm within the cells of a living leaf or plant, which is the part of the photosynthesis process responding to energy from the sun.

The Kirlian photography, originally developed in Russia, and now accepted internationally, also reveals the same process in plants, but goes further. It photographs glowing color and sparks and flashes, coming from the hands of people as well as other parts of the body.* This type of photography is now being studied in various universities.

An article in *Newsweek*, March 4, 1974 stated:

In Kirlian photography, named after the Russian husband-and-wife team of S. D. and V. Kirlian who developed it in 1939, the object to be photographed—usually a human finger—is placed in direct contact with the emulsion of an ordinary photographic film in a pitch-black room. Extensive research in recent years has shown that the shape, size and color of the corona (aura) seem to depend on the mood of the subject at the moment that his fingerprint is photographed. When the average person is calm, his Kirlian corona is small, subdued and pale blue. But if that same subject is roused to anger, the corona generally flares up with brilliant reds and oranges.

Such information provides photographic proof that living matter *does* radiate its own form of electromagnetic energy. It also proves that after exposure to certain colors, *something* happens to plants, and, as we shall soon learn, to people, too. Skeptics can no longer claim that the effect of color is a mere figment of the imagination.

In the case of the effect of light and color, Dr. Ott says, "Inasmuch as light is the source of energy that brings about these chemical changes, it then seems reasonable to assume that by changing the characteristics of the light energy, the resulting chemical changes would likewise be altered."

After finding out that different colors affected plants differently, Dr. Ott next applied his microscope time-lapse cameras to animal cells to see

---

* Sheila Ostrander and Lynn Schroeder: *Psychic Discoveries Behind the Iron Curtain.* Bantam Books, New York, sixth printing, 1971

what would happen there. He reported, "Microscopic time-lapse pictures of many different animal cells in tissue culture also show variations of growth patterns when different colored filters are placed in the photographic light source."

As we have already discovered, there are some forms of radiation, even in the form of color, which must be chosen judiciously. On the positive side, Dr. Ott reports that fish in the Miami Seaquarium, with a disease called "pop-eye," were cured by exposure to ultraviolet light fifteen minutes daily for five days. He also learned that employees working in the Well of the Sea Restaurant in Chicago's Hotel Sherman House had almost never had colds or suffered from viruses. The Well of the Sea had been lighted for seventeen years with near-black ultraviolet light. Dr. Ott states, "The longer wavelengths of ultraviolet that penetrate the atmosphere at intensities comparable to visible light are sometimes referred to as near-ultraviolet, and include the so-called black-light-ultraviolet." (Apparently this is safe.) He adds, "The shorter wavelengths of ultraviolet . . . are sometimes referred to as far-ultraviolet, and include the germicidal wavelengths that can be very harmful."

Since the black ultraviolet of the restaurant is within the safe limits, it produced good results only. There are also examples of other good effects of long-wave ultraviolet (as from the sun, used for short periods only for safety). Luckiesh and Pacini write:

Prominent observers seemed to have established that ultraviolet radiation applied to the surface of the body can benefit calcium metabolism. . . . Ultraviolet is also apparently specific in its effect upon the sympathetic nervous system through which intermediary its stimulus is carried to every cell of the living organism, inciting to action at the same time the whole glandular mechanism and the gonads [sex organs].

On the other hand, as we now know, too much ultraviolet can cause trouble. Ultraviolet sunlamps may cause serious burns and eye damage; too much sun exposure at the wrong time of day for many people can result in severe sunburn. Levy and Passoul found that an excess of ultraviolet can even cause internal trouble. Rats exposed to an overdose of ultraviolet radiation, and later autopsied, were found to have marked engorgement in many of their internal organs, especially the liver, spleen and lungs.

Remember this when you are tempted to suntan hour after hour. Add this effect to the aging of skin, skin cancer, and sun stroke, and learn to develop a respect for ultraviolet, which can be your friend in helping to improve your health when used in moderation, but your foe when used without caution or restraint.

Another wavelength that comes in color, and which can be dangerous, is infrared (heat-producing). Infrared, like ultraviolet, occurs in sunlight, and can also burn. The proportions of infrared and ultraviolet in solar radiations reaching the earth vary with atmospheric conditions. Infrared lamps are often used for physiotherapy. However, infrared must be used with caution. Some dogs get cataracts when their eyes are continuously exposed to the infrared rays of an open fireplace. I have at least one friend who swears that every time she stands near an infrared heat lamp used to keep food hot at a restaurant, she becomes ill. Maybe so.

There is definite proof of danger in some other types of radiant energy. Luckiesh and Pacini explain:

X-rays and the gamma rays of r⸱ᵈium produce many changes of the blood. Blood platelets are rapidly diminished in number when the body is exposed to X-rays and the gamma rays even when the quantity of X-rays used is insufficient to produce any apparent effect upon the red-cell and the hemoglobin content. With more prolonged exposures the platelet count drops so low that it never again recovers and when this happens the animal always dies from an intercurrent infection. . . .

X-rays and gamma rays are foreign to the natural environment . . . furnished in excess, X-rays lead to a severe disintegration of the skin and its underlying muscle which is most difficult to heal. A large ulcerating surface is produced. (The destructive effects of the X-rays on the skin have in many instances been overcome by the constructive effect of the ultraviolet radiation played on the ulcerating surface.)

X-rays have also been cited as causing some forms of cancer.* Cobalt rays are controversial. Some medical researchers believe that though they destroy malignant cells, they destroy the good cells along with the bad.

Another possible hazard is TV, especially color TV. According to Dr. Ott, alarming results from exposure to color TV have been noted with both animals and people. Radioactivity can result from a colored TV set backed up to a wall, on the opposite side of which is a baby's crib. Hyperkinetic

* Griffiths, Joel & Ballantine, Richard: *Silent Slaughter*, Regnery, Chicago, 1972

children as well as animals have been observed after exposure. As Griffiths and Ballantine say in their book *Silent Slaughter,** "A television is a low-voltage X-ray machine." Dr. Ott adds, "The reason why color TV is more dangerous than black and white, is because it emits a higher voltage of radiation . . . it is not color itself which is harmful from a TV color set. It is the fact that the potential source of X-rays of a color TV set is equal to that of watching three black and white sets at the same time."

One woman reported that three cats died from sleeping on top of her color TV while it was turned on. All of this information is explained and documented in my book, *Are You Radioactive?†*

The colors in color therapy are not only considered effective but safe. William Benham Snow, M.D., says:

Radiant light and heat and color are capable of setting up responsive vibrations in animal tissue, inducing responses relative to their intensity.

It is readily appreciated that those various frequencies of color vibrations, affecting, as they do, human tissue, induce effects relative to their wave lengths and frequencies. Under varying conditions it will be readily appreciated that the judicious employment of the wide range of vibratory radiant energy will be in a large measure capable either of restoring or inhibiting the vibratory energies or activities of the animal or human organism.

Now let us look at some results of the use of color.

* Ibid.
† Linda Clark: *Are You Radioactive? How to Protect Yourself,* The Devin-Adair Co., Old Greenwich, Conn., 1973

4. The Psychological
Impact of Color

The Pittsburgh Plate Glass Company, in its booklet, *Color Dynamics For The Home,* provides the following general information on how to utilize the energy of color:

Color is in no way an experiment. Its principles have been widely tested in many fields with uniformly beneficial results. Laboratory tests and practical experience prove that there is energy in color which affects your health, comfort, happiness and safety.

When our color engineers started their study of the use of color in industry, educational institutions, office buildings and homes, they were determined to explore the physiological and psychological reactions and benefits in these various fields of operation.

Their conclusions were that these results are due to the *energy* in color. Color, in the form of light, is part of the electro-magnetic spectrum. Light is one of its many octaves; others are cosmic rays, gamma rays, X-rays, ultraviolet rays, infrared rays, radio and television rays—including light—all possessing energy.

Variations in the number of impacts upon the eye affect muscular, mental and nervous activity. For example, tests show that under ordinary light muscular activity is twenty-three empirical units. It advances slightly under blue light. Green light increases it a little more. Yellow light raises it to thirty units. Subject a person to a given color for as little as five minutes and his mental as well as his muscular activity changes.

The medical profession has long realized that colors can be used to stimulate or depress. Some help people relax and be cheerful. Others stimulate and invigorate them. Still others set up irritation and actual physical discomfort.

Originally developed to increase efficiency in industry, its use has accomplished results in scores of large factories that are truly phenomenal. Testimonials tell how this science reduces workers' eye fatigue, lifts spirits, improves quality and quantity in production. Accidents are reduced.

Its use in hospitals has speeded the recovery of patients; effectiveness of medical and nursing staffs has been raised.

In schools concentration is assisted, energy stimulated, eye fatigue retarded among students and teachers alike. Leading hotels have utilized color dynamics to impart an atmosphere of friendliness, comfort and good cheer. Offices are made to seem more spacious, pleasing to the eyes, contributing to the health and efficiency of employees.

Even color schemes in planes are chosen to provide adequate light-reflection to counteract claustrophobia and help eliminate air sickness. Colors are also chosen for spaciousness, stability, as well as to encourage intestinal fortitude and equilibrium and dispel sea sickness on ocean liners.

COLOR IN INDUSTRY

Corinne Heline, in her book, *Color and Music in the New Age,* gives examples of the psychological effects of color.

In a London factory, absenteeism among women was soaring at an alarming rate. A color specialist found that blue color lighting made the women look sickly, especially when they looked into the mirror. This caused them to actually feel ill. When a warm beige was painted over the iron gray walls, the effect of the blue lighting was neutralized and the absenteeism was no longer a problem.

In another factory, gray machines were painted a light orange. Morale improved, accidents decreased, and formerly disgruntled employees began to sing while they worked.*

In a factory cafeteria, which was air-conditioned and had light blue walls, the employees complained of the cold though the temperature was 72°. Some employees even wore their coats to meals. Later, when the temperature was raised to 75°, the employees still shivered and complained. Finally a color consultant advised repainting the walls orange. The employees then complained that the 75° temperature was too warm. Finally it was reduced to the original 72° and everyone was happy again.*

People tend to overestimate the passage of time in a red room, and underestimate it in a green room. Two groups of salesmen whose watches had been removed were asked to guess how long a meeting had lasted. In the red room, the men guessed six hours, whereas the meeting lasted only three hours. In the green room the men thought they had spent less time than they actually had.

The average person will judge a dark-colored

* Roland T. Hunt: *Complete Color Prescription*. Devorss and Co., Los Angeles, 1962

object to be heavier than a light-colored one. In a plant in which briar pipes were packed in black metal boxes, the workers insisted the boxes were so heavy they strained their backs. But when the foreman had the same boxes painted green, the workers commented on the light weight of the "new" boxes.

COLOR AND SUICIDE

Red impels people to action; green (the color of nature) seems to promote a feeling of well-being. Black can be depressing. Blackfriars Bridge in London, with its black iron work, was famous for its many suicides. When the bridge was re-painted green, the suicides declined more than a third. (San Franciscans, please take note: your Golden Gate Bridge, also notorious for multitudinous suicides, is painted red which, as already pointed out, impels people to action. Try green!)

COLOR IN HOSPITALS AND INSTITUTIONS

Color has a definite influence in hospitals and institutions. In a federal narcotic rehabilitation institution located in Texas, patients were moved from one colored room to another to spend their emotional recovery. Bright yellows and oranges are being used in the University of California, San Francisco Medical Center hospital rooms. These bright warm colors, particularly in the intensive care units, are found to make patients feel more cheerful and want to get well faster.

Roland T. Hunt tells of corresponding many years ago with Sister Kenny who said that she was using color as well as hydrotherapy to stimulate muscular response in polio cases. She felt it was invaluable in helping to restore body control. Mr. Hunt states:

It has been proved that certain shades used in hospital wards and operating rooms can calm nerves and restore vitality. A hospital in St. Albans, England, was one of the first to adopt color. In the Manhattan Eye, Ear and Throat Hospital, white was replaced with a non-glare blue for operating theatres, operating gowns and sheets. It should be possible in all hospitals to flood walls of private and ward rooms with courageous tones of color for those fearing forthcoming operations; recuperative tones for the convalescent; sedative tones for the excitable; and stimulative tones for those who suffer the depths of mental depression.

Mr. Hunt describes a hospital recovery room where patients were coming out of anesthesia, crying and moaning. When Mr. Hunt set up a machine which projected colors onto the ceiling, absolute silence resulted.

C. E. Iredell, M.D., a London surgeon who had had long experience with color on his patients, stated that there is no question but that color can increase the resistance of a hospital patient.*

Blue is an emotionally sedative color and is used in hospital recovery rooms following surgery. It is also used to quiet violent patients in mental institutions.

COLOR IN SCHOOLS

The right color can even boost school grades, according to one instructor at San Francisco State

----

* Ibid.

College. His theory is that comprehension and re-call of difficult subject matter in school can be improved by using photographic slides in color rather than black and white. Nearly every college student has fallen asleep in a dim lecture hall when lights go out and graphs and other tables are flashed on the screen. The San Francisco College Instructor, Richard J. Michael, who has been experimenting with color in the college department of Design and Industry, found, by testing students after lectures were over, that single color slides proved most effective if the color were a cool green. Next best was red, then blue.

When green slides were used, test scores rose as much as forty percent above exposure to ordinary black-and-white slides. Two-color slides of red and green produced test scores of more than twice as high as black-and-white. Three-color visual aids—red and green on a blue background—increased the test scores thirty percent.

COLOR IN SPORTS

Color in sports can also be helpful. Alonzo Stagg, while he was head coach at Chicago, had two dressing rooms for his players. One was painted blue for rest periods; the other was painted red for fight talks. The athletic director at University of New Mexico decorated his own football team dressing room with red and that of the visiting opponent team in blue. (Colors on the red side of the spectrum are considered stimulating, whereas the blues and greens are cool and relaxing.)

Felicia Fuller, a color psychologist for a paint

company, believes that baseballs should be a bright
coral red; golf balls any bright color except white;
and the ice in hockey rinks should be tinted a
pale green. And in hockey, the object which is
the puck should be red or green, instead of a drab
black, since the eye follows a color more easily.

How Color Can Influence People

Color association with certain products has an
effect on the buyer. Red toothbrushes are avoided
(because they suggest bleeding!). Amber is more
successful and sells better.*

Felicia Fuller predicts that color dynamics are
going to be a powerful factor in our lives. People
can be influenced by color. A factory which painted
its drinking fountain area a nice soft green attracted dawdlers. When it was repainted a vivid
orange, workers got their drink and left immediately.

A UPI report, July 26, 1967, stated:

Howard Ketchum, color psychologist and designer,
president of his color-design firm with offices in New
York, Zurich and Munich, recommends colored sidewalks for cities. Ketchum has been using color to influence behavior for more than three decades.

When a bus company asked him how a new design
and color could make riders want to step to the rear
of the vehicles, he recommended making the rear section like a plane's cocktail lounge—open and brightly
colored. His suggestion proved workable. To get people to move to the rear of the elevator he prescribes
painting the back wall a contrasting and inviting
color. Around schools, he believes a golden yellow

* Ibid.

pigment added to the concrete in the sidewalks would be helpful, since yellow, he says, is the best cerebral stimulating color. It is also sunshiny and cheerful.

Vera Stanley Alder, a portrait painter as well as a researcher in ancient wisdom, tells us that color is registered by the optic nerves, and medical science has proved that different colors have very definite effects upon our nervous systems. She says, "Dark, drab and dingy colors harm our spirits, morale, and health; they encourage crime, inhibitions, inferiority complexes, suicide and stunted development. They actually prevent the radiation of personal magnetism, and give-and-take between human beings. They inhibit optimism, inspiration and therefore success."*

COLORS IN CLOTHES

A study conducted at Pennsylvania State University reported that college girls who were secure chose neutral colors (grays and beige) and fewer warm colors, whereas girls who were less self-confident preferred brighter colors and very light or very dark shades.

Buying a color which becomes you is important, but choosing a color to wear on a certain day to compensate for the way you feel is also important. I experienced this after moving from New York to California, where the sun shines most of the time. Several years later I was required to spend three winter months once again in the suburbs of New York City. The landscape was drab; the

* Vera Stanley Alder: *The Finding of the Third Eye.* Samuel Weiser, Inc., Third Impression, New York, 1972

trees were leafless; the weather was unpleasant. Everything looked depressing and I felt the cold intensely after the warmth of California. One day I went into New York City and indulged in a red buying spree. I bought a red dress, a red coat, a red nightie and a red robe. I wore them almost constantly while I was in the New York area that winter. After returning to warm, sunny California I have seldom worn them since.

The owner of a dress shop tells me she chooses her own daily costume color according to the way she feels when she gets up. If she is full of energy she wears a more subdued color. If she feels the need for more energy, she picks a bright color. If her morale is low, she chooses white.

Raymond Twyeffort, a fashion tailor formerly of Rockefeller Center in New York City, and a past president of the National Association of Merchant Tailors of America, with a business in six figures, has long believed in the effect of color, and started applying it to men's clothes as early as 1928.

Mr. Twyeffort felt that if color is used freely, it may cure dyspepsia as well as feelings of inferiority and discouragement. His first observation of color was on himself. When he was young, he suffered from stomach trouble, yet his doctors found no explanation. He also feared cars, trains and paved streets. One day he donned a scarlet hunting coat, and felt so exhilarated that he began wearing colored ties, vests and pajamas. His fears not only vanished, his stomach troubles also disappeared and he suddenly realized that color had been responsible for the changes.

He began to apply his theories to men's clothes. He believes red makes a man strong, dynamic and courageous; yellow makes him feel happy and carefree; orange helps him to be assertive; green encourages stability; and blue is soothing. For those men who demand a black suit, he agonizes, "Black, death, sorrow!"

Mr. Twyeffort then decided that color could help the aged. He told older people that color would help their gait to become firmer; their eyes brighter. And before long, they did indeed seem to feel better.

One of his aging clients was an 84-year-old man who began to feel more frisky when he acquired a midnight blue suit, and later one made of sea-foam green. The man finally adventurously chose, with Twyeffort's help, an orange dinner jacket which he wore with a yellow vest and a scarlet cummerbund. He felt so rejuvenated that he bought a large Cadillac and began driving it himself.*

So Women's Lib is now being applied to men!

Thousands of other people, like Mr. Twyeffort's client, are turning to color as a means of transforming their personalities, according to an article in *The Wall Street Journal* (August 6, 1973). To find out which colors are most effective for them, they are seeking the help of professional color consultants to help them find individual key colors for wardrobes, home furnishing and even cars.

One personal color consultant in San Francisco says that his business just about doubles each year; another has assembled personal color palettes for 200,000 clients in 33 Western cities since she began in 1942. Prices for these consultations range from low to high, but those who have been

* Roland T. Hunt: *Complete Color Prescription*. Devorss and Co., Los Angeles, 1962

counselled swear that color has changed their
lives. Many people insist that they have more
confidence, get better jobs, more friends, and have
occasionally even saved a broken marriage. Perhaps, because they look better in colors chosen to
enhance their appearance, their attitude is improved psychologically, and such changes are possible.

This type of color consultation, however, is restricted to colors chosen to blend with the individual's appearance only. It may not be dependable in affecting their physical state.

There is a fascinating do-it-yourself color test
now available which gives psychological information through a person's choices and rejections
of colors. This test is simple, and fun, but definitely not a parlor game. It was developed by Dr.
Max Lüscher, a university professor of psychology.
Dr. Lüscher first presented this color test to an
international medical conference in Lausanne,
Switzerland, in 1947. Since then the test has been
widely studied and used throughout Europe by
psychologists to learn accurate psychological information about patients, and by physicians to
uncover such medical information as the functioning of the glandular system. Industry is also
using this test to screen job applicants. Dr. Lüscher has been employed as a color consultant for
pharmaceutical companies. He also helped to
choose the colors for all the Volkswagen plants in
West Germany.

The Lüscher Color Test is described in a book
of the same name*, by an English writer, Ian A.

* Ian A. Scott: *The Lüscher Color Test* (based on the original
German text by Dr. Max Lüscher). Random House, New York,
1969. (Paperback Edition, Pocket Books, New York, 1971)

Scott, who, after a career in aviation, has now turned to a second career in health and physical fitness. Mr. Scott's interest in psychological factors which underlie ill health led him to study, use and write about the Lüscher color test and its benefits. His book presents the test, how it works, and even includes color charts so that you can try out a simple form of the test for yourself, your family and friends. Professionals can use the information in the book in a more technical form as a "deep" psychological test to administer to their patients. People who tell me they have tried this test informally have been surprised at its accuracy. But more important is the scientific basis which underlies the color test, showing that there is a real scientific need for the use and effect of color in our lives.

Today we need color more than at any time in history. Blacks and grays, both depressing, should be replaced with colors of inspiration, tranquility and happiness, both in clothes and offices, as well as in homes where people spend so many hours a day.

It was Dr. Ott who said, "The effect of color is not merely psychological. It is necessary to think of color as wave lengths of radiant energy."

Now let us look at what the radiant energy of color can do to help physical health.

5. Color and Physical Health

In her book, *Healing and Regeneration Through Color,** Corinne Heline writes:

Color dynamics are in no way an experiment. The principles have been widely tested in many fields with uniformly beneficial results.

Colors are effective as a cure for disease and may even add ten years to the life of a human being, according to Lord Clifford of Chudleigh, who has studied the action of light shades on vegetable growth for many years. He believes that every disease can be cured by certain colors. Yellow is the restorer of nerves, he finds, while green increases vitality.

He says, "One shade of red is the most effectual in all cases of blood poisoning. . . .

"A particular shade of violet causes the growth of bone; and indigo produces muscular generation and strength.

"Then there is the shade of green which produces vitality and general energy of the system and also the growth of fat; yellow restores the nerves. But of course the greatest care should be taken that only the right shade is used or opposite results may be obtained.

"The treatment would also benefit most people suf-

---

* Bowery Press, Santa Barbara, tenth edition, 1964

fering from premature old age and mental worry produced by past illness. It could well add ten years to their lives. I do not claim that it can make people of sixty feel like thirty-five, but it can certainly restore them to the state of activity enjoyed a dozen years before."

C. G. Sander, in his book, *Color In Health and Disease,** states that when the body is in a normal condition, it may be able to filter out from the white light (or sunlight) whatever color vibration it needs. However, according to Sander, if a person is not in normal health, the necessary color must be supplied.

Whatever the explanation of how it works, S.G.J. Ouseley says, "There is every reason to believe that the use of color in the treatment of disease may at some period not far distant take its place as a recognized science."

R. Brooks Simpkins, a successful color practitioner for eye problems in England for many years, adds, "It has been prophesied that the day will come when doctors will prescribe visible rays instead of medicine—rays of different wave lengths according to the nature of the illness."

As stated before, color therapy is not new. In the golden age of Greece as well as in the healing temples of light in Egypt, color healing was used with success. The Pythagoreans were probably the first to experiment with color therapy, using even then the principle that it could be fed through the eyes to the body. Therefore, the most recent findings of the effect of color and light cannot be called "new"—they are merely rediscovered.

* C. W. Daniel Co., London, 1926

So far we have learned that there are different methods of applying light (which contains colors). It can be received through the skin, or the eyes, where, in turn, it has been found to stimulate certain internal glands.

The late Colonel Dinshah P. Ghadiali, a former medical practitioner in India who later became a resident of the United States, was, and still is, considered the outstanding color researcher of the world. Although ancient cultures used color therapy routinely, Dinshah, as he was called, did more recent exhaustive research and testing and made his findings available for practical use today. He called color therapy, "Spectro-Chrome Therapy." He discovered that certain specific colors influenced specific glands:

STIMULANT WAVE	GLAND
Red	Liver
Orange	Thyroid
Orange	Mammary
Yellow	Choroid
Lemon	Pancreas
Lemon	Thymus
Green	Pituitary
Blue	Pineal
Indigo	Parathyroid
Violet	Spleen
Magenta	Suprarenals
Magenta	Prostate
Scarlet	Testicle
Scarlet	Ovary

As Corinne Heline testifies, "Concentration of the specific color needed will stimulate the secretion of the gland corresponding to the color, and the flow will aid the parts of the body affected."

Dr. N. S. Hanoka, a color researcher in India adds:

Color waves applied to the body are individually potent for therapeutic measures. There are no disagreeable side effects such as artificial sunburn or blistering from ultraviolet lamps; no destruction of tissues as in X-ray therapy and the use of radium; no removal of anatomical structures as in surgery; and it relieves pain by removing the cause instead of deadening the brain centers as in drug therapy.

For the relief of pain alone, color therapy is invaluable. But the prevention of disease conditions far exceeds its other virtues. Color can be applied to a particular area to relieve a certain symptom. It works precisely on the organ to which it is applied and the beneficial effects so consistently obtained warrant a confidence that cannot be placed in any other known method. By treating organs through certain skin areas, or tuning up the different endocrine glands and stimulating the lymphatic system for better drainage, areas of decomposed tissue and bacteria are cleaned out of the body—not only acute infection conditions, but chronic foci as well. Along with this there is an elimination of toxic substances which obstruct normal functions. . . . Thus, the organism as a whole, is not only relieved of its present burden, but raised to a high level of resistance, which enables it to cope with future trouble in a way that was not previously possible.

Dr. Hanoka concludes, "Color therapy is universally applicable to all the ills to which the human flesh is heir."

Here is one example: A baby was born with a blood defect, a dangerously low bilirubin (a derivative of hemoglobin) count. Doctors decided there were two alternatives possible to save its life: an exchange transfusion, or phototherapy treatment (exposure to bright light or sunlight). The baby had already developed signs of blood incompatibility and the mother did not wish to risk an exchange transfusion which could be fatal to her child. So she requested phototherapy, which was described by Dr. J. A. Lucey in the medical journal, *Pediatric* (Vol. 41, 1968), as "simple, inexpensive and safe." The baby was given phototherapy treatment by a nurse who was experienced in color therapy. After five days under blue light the baby made a complete recovery, developed normally with vigorous growth and became a contented, healthy baby.*

The late Dr. Oscar Brunler, who died in 1952, was one of the most illustrious practitioners of color therapy. A Scandinavian physicist, he became an English citizen during World War II and received the Bessemer Prize in Physics for his many inventions, one of which was used in the Normandy landing. Rather than take part in nuclear weaponry, he decided to abandon physics and study medicine. After taking his degree and becoming associated with a London hospital, he became an expert in color therapy, lectured widely on the subject and wrote four books. He cited some fascinating studies and case histories which he observed during his practice, including the following:

Animals put in different colored boxes were tested. They lost vitality due to exposure to one color and were revitalized with exposure to another.

In describing the use of yellow-orange, Dr. Brunler reported that he had radiated the livers

---

* *Awake* Magazine, November 22, 1970, p. 12

of diabetics with yellow-orange and, as a result, the intake of insulin was lowered from 145 units of insulin previously required daily, to 25 units.

A group of men were partially intoxicated. Some of them were then subjected to yellow-orange light, the others to red. Those exposed to red light continued to drink. Those exposed to yellow-orange refused further alcohol.

A well-known actress from Scotland came to London. She had lost her voice and other doctors had told her she could not appear on the stage for six weeks. Dr. Brunler radiated her body with yellow-orange, both on the liver area as well as her vocal cords, and her voice became normal in forty minutes.

In another patient, an inflamed appendix cleared up in nine minutes after a red light of certain frequency was beamed upon it.

Dr. Brunler reports the effect of red blankets in various hospitals. In the Balkans, smallpox patients wrapped in red blankets recovered without scarring. In India, in one hospital, red blankets were used to speed post-operative healing. The doctor in charge had once been a chronic sufferer of hives when he was a child. His mother had wrapped him in a red blanket and put him to bed. After a few hours, the hives had cleared up.

A man came for treatment to Dr. Brunler at his London office one morning at 9:30 A.M. While the man was in the office, his wife phoned from their Norfolk, England, home to say that their four-year-old child was dying from an asthmatic attack. An injection given by a local doctor had had no effect; the child was having serious trouble breathing and had turned blue.

Dr. Brunler told the man to tell the mother to put a red silk ribbon around their daughter's left wrist. The father argued against it, but finally gave in and telephoned Dr. Brunler's information to his wife.

At 11:30 A.M. the mother phoned that the child was breathing normally. By 1:30 P.M. she called the office to say that the child was sitting up eating. By evening the child was back to normal, but Dr. Brunler advised her wearing the red ribbon for a while longer.

In case you question such stories, Dr. Brunler explains that red, measuring 6500 A.U., penetrates five-eighths of an inch into the body. A beam of red light has split a "form C" salt crystal on contact. We cannot get around the fact that a color, each with its own frequency, *is a form of energy*. (More explanations of why colors are so successful appear in chapter nine on individual colors.)

Dr. Brunler says that when we speak of color, we are speaking of energy waves. He adds, "Colors are far more powerful than medicine."

Edwin D. Babbitt, M.D., explained it as follows: "Any process, light or heat, that draws blood to the skin relieves congestion of liver, spleen, lungs, stomach, intestines and spinal cord. All vital organs have direct connection with the skin through the arteries, blood vessels and capillaries. Application of light rays in one spot can affect the entire blood stream through circulation and elimination of toxins.

"Incandescent lights and colors heal by stimulation, oxidation of toxins, and vitalization, allowing nature to produce healing. Freund, of Germany, used them for skin diseases, neuralgia, rheumatism, muscle soreness, swelling joints and muscles."

This makes sense in treating specific areas. But I, personally, still could not quite understand why color should contribute to better health in general, until I discovered something which rang a bell: *color is also a form of nourishment or nutrition!* This came as a distinct surprise to me.

Dr. Edwin D. Babbitt listed the elements found in the sun's atmosphere which have been discovered by means of the spectroscope. They can be absorbed by body exposure or by ingesting foods. Here is his list of twenty important elements, including sixteen metals or minerals plus four additional elements: oxygen, hydrogen, nitrogen and carbon. The minerals are: sodium, calcium, barium, magnesium, iron, chromium, nickel, copper, zinc, strontium, cadmium, cobalt, manganese, aluminum, titanium and rubidium.

So either nutrition or light can supply energy. Combining them strengthens the use of each. William Benham Snow, M.D., believed that color therapy could help restore health, and good nutrition could help maintain it. Dr. Babbitt agrees. He said, "Long repeated color therapy treatment *plus* proper diet produces wonders."

The next chapter explains why this is so.

6. Color and Nutrition

Food is still another means of introducing sunlight and color into the body. The 1961 Nobel Prize in chemistry was awarded to Dr. Melvin Calvin, of the University of California, for his work in unravelling the complicated steps in photosynthesis. This is the process in which the green pigment in plants—chlorophyl—harnesses the energy of sunlight to synthesize carbohydrates from carbon dioxide in the air, water and soil. Dr. Calvin was able to identify each element created in the plant, step by step, at all stages of growth, until the final products, starches and sugars, were manufactured.

A bulletin from the University of California states, "Photosynthesis has been called the most important chemical process on earth because it is responsible for the oxygen that we breathe and the food we eat. During photosynthesis green plants trap the sun's energy and transform it into chemical energy. This chemical energy is then used by the plant to convert carbon dioxide and water into carbohydrates, protein and fats. These are stored in the plants for use by the higher forms of life." Someone has described chlorophyl in the vegetable kingdom as the equivalent of blood of the human system.

Analyses show that fruit, picked green, does not develop the full potential flavor or vitamins and minerals as that which is allowed to ripen on the tree, or even which, once picked, ripens in natural sunlight.

George A. Wilson, D.C., former Chief Emeritus of Spears Chiropractic Hospital, Research Department, and the author of several fascinating books based on his research, recommends that one's diet should have a preponderance of vegetables, grown above ground, which *carry imprisoned sunlight*. The Orientals agree. They say, "Eat three parts of foods grown above ground to one grown below the ground." They believe this balance contributes to health, apparently because these foods are more accessible to sunlight.

Luckiesh and Pacini state:

Each food derived from natural vegetation is, in the last analysis, a condensation of products built up by the light of the sun, which the natural forces of the body liberate from foods imprisoned by solar energy. Our own animation is an exhibition of the release of energy from the multitude of products which we term food.

At one time foreigners living in certain districts of New York City used to make their spaghetti at home, using flour and water, and occasionally egg for noodles. Spaghetti and noodles were looped over broom handles and placed out on the fire escapes to dry. Later fire ordinances required no obstructions allowed on the fire escapes and forced the drying of spaghetti indoors. Within three months after this change the veteran spaghetti eaters noted a depreciation in the nutritive content as well as a loss of satisfying quality of the product. Not until later did Steenbock, a researcher, report that there was fact behind this observation. Flour, edible oils, including olive oil and cod liver oil, become more nourishing after exposure to ultraviolet radiation. Other products which become receptacles for ultraviolet radiation, according to Steenbock's experiments are yeast, commercial casein, bile, lanoline, whole grains and their products such as starch, meals, flours, oils and cereals. Thus, such food treated, can become bottled or solidified sunshine.

Certain preservatives such as benzoate derivatives (benzoic acid, sodium benzoate, etc.) apparently destroy the active qualities of irradiated fats, and may interfere with natural properties which vegetables grown in the sunlight should normally possess. The radiation provided by sunlight may impart the touch of nature which, when obeyed, furnishes the open sesame to the miracle of life.

VITAMINS AND COLOR

It is known that sunlight is a source of vitamin D. Doctors who prescribe cod liver oil (which contains vitamin D) to prevent rickets in children, formerly discontinued the use of oil during the summer when the children are exposed to the sun. Now, due to smog and fog in some communities, cod liver oil is recommended the year around.

Animals, either fur or feather bearing, expose themselves to the sun, and either lick their fur or preen their feathers to take into their bodies the vitamin D captured in the oil on fur or feathers. Humans manufacture vitamin D in the oil of their skin wherever clothes are not present. Even if all-over sunbaths are not possible, it is said that factory workers who eat their lunch out of doors can acquire sufficient vitamin D on the skin of their faces, necks and arms during the lunch hours to fulfill their nutritional need of vitamin D. Incidentally, it is best not to bathe in water immediately after sunbathing. The vitamin D is washed off the skin before the body can absorb it.

In Russia a study was conducted of 94 children with rickets. Treatment included vitamin D, remedial exercises daily, and ultraviolet radiation every second day in increasing amounts. Calcium-phosphorus ratios, bone conditions, even catarrh of the upper respiratory tract reached near normal under this treatment.

Since food is a form of imprisoned sunlight, vitamin D is not the only vitamin found in solarized food. Other vitamins have been detected and *have been correlated with certain colors.*

The following colors are attributed to vitamins: Vitamin A is yellow. Vitamin B-12 is red (other B vitamins are included in red and orange colors). Vitamin C is lemon colored. Vitamin D is violet. Vitamin E is scarlet. Vitamin K is indigo. Therefore, most yellow foods are rich in vitamin A. Yellow and green foods are usually rich in vitamin C. Yellow and orange foods often contain both vitamins.

S.G.J. Ouseley in his book, *The Power of the Rays,** writes, "One of the best ways of absorbing color is the judicious use of vegetables, fruit, and liquids which have been sun-charged. Fruits and vegetables are the direct result of the sun's radiation."

Dr. Ernest Stevens adds, "The dietetic rate for foods has been well studied, but not their vibra-

* London, L. N. Fowler, Ltd., fourth edition, 1963

tory value. Each food vibrates at its own rate, and entering the body modifies the body's rate. If it is a disharmonic rate, the rate of the body is disturbed and interfered with, and discord issues from this disagreement. Also by our vibratory rates at the time we eat, determined by our thoughts or feelings (i.e., anger), we modify the food rates for good or evil.

". . . There should, in eating, be a regard for colors of foods . . . That is the electronic color-vibratory rate . . . In cooking or overcooking we often kill the vital color."

PHYSICAL EFFECTS OF NATURALLY COLORED FOODS

Dr. Bernard Jensen makes these suggestions: yellow fruits and vegetables such as corn, squash and peaches, are laxative foods. Deep red foods, such as beets and dark cherries, are blood builders. Green foods such as spinach, green beans, kale, chinese cabbage, parsley, beet greens and Swiss chard, are body mineralizers. Beet juice combined with blackberry juice is a good blood builder. Thus, following Dr. Jensen, naturally colored foods are a good means of getting color into the body for health improvement.

Natural beverages are still another method of utilizing color. Vegetables and fruit juices, of course, carry the color and qualities of the vegetable or fruit into their juices. But water can also be a means of stored sunlight. Many people place ordinary water in a gallon jug, with a cork or cap, and place it in the sunlight for at least twelve hours, or more. It seems to purify the water and improve the taste, by exposure to the sun. Edwin D. Babbitt, M.D., who practiced color therapy in the last century, writes:

Light being an actual substance moving with peculiar styles of vibrations according to the particular colors which compose it, and at a rate of nearly 186,000 miles a second, it is easy to see that it must have great power, and that the substances receiving it must partake of this power. The fact that the whole world, mineral, vegetable and animal, is ever being transformed into new and beautiful growths, forms and colors under its magic touch, shows its almost omnific power.

Reichenbach [another color researcher] let water stand in the sunlight for five minutes, then a highly sensitive assistant, on drinking it without knowing what was done, said immediately that it was magnetized. It produced a peculiar pepper-like burning on her tongue, palate and throat, down to the stomach, at every point arousing spasmodic symptoms.

Water which stood in the sun twenty minutes was found to be as strongly magnetic as if it had been charged with a nine-layered magnet. Another M.D. who put water in a clear bottle in the sunshine for two days was astonished at the burning quality of the water, a reaction which remained the same during following tests.

But many go one step further. By putting water in a sunny window, with the colored filter between the sun and the water, or into a colored glass, jar or bottle, and placing it in the sun, they believe it is possible to transfer the effect of the colored wavelengths to the water itself.

Dr. Babbitt says, "Water can be color-charged somewhat within an hour indoors. I allow the colored filters to hang in the window where the sunlight can strike the containers, meantime putting in fresh water every three or four days in hot weather to keep it pure. I have tested the power of water charged with colored lenses in hundreds of cases, generally with the same effect."

I know one woman and her husband who manufacture "red" water and "blue" water regularly for their own use. They have constructed a simple wooden partitioned cabinet. Inside, on a shelf on one side, which is an open frame with an edge only, they have put a red glass pane; on the other side, a blue pane. Above these glass panes are sockets for 100-watt light bulbs. Under each pane of glass is room for a wide-mouthed gallon jar (ordinarily used by restaurants for mayonnaise, pickles, etc.).

My friends turn on the lights over the water-filled jars, with the red rays shining on one, the blue on the other, and leave them under the light for twelve hours. They then use the "red" water or "blue" water to drink or make beverages. For instance, they make their morning coffee from the stimulating "red" water. Toward the end of the day they use the "blue" water for more sedative effects. They also apply the "blue" water for insect bites and other skin irritations.

Another friend puts water in colored glasses or jars and sets them in the sun for varying lengths of time before drinking. She has acquired a collection of colored tumblers, in case she wishes to color-solarize only a small amount of water quickly. For larger amounts, she has a collection of larger colored jars and bottles.

NATURAL VS. SYNTHETIC FOODS

Synthetic foods are not nourished by the sun. Anthropologists have found that tribes the world over who subsisted on natural food remained healthy for their life span. When these same or other tribes turned to synthetic foods, their health suffered proportionately. This is especially true for the Eskimos.

It is obvious that the more intense the color of the food, the better, since not only is the color more concentrated, but also indicates a higher vitamin/mineral content. This may explain why naturally green celery and asparagus are nutritionally richer than the white, bleached varieties. One color expert of my acquaintance has worked with colors so long that she says she automatically "cooks in color." She feels she cannot serve a proper meal unless it is color-balanced with all colors present. If a color is missing, she supplies it with decorative fruit or flowers on the table, the color of which can at least be taken into the body through the eye, as Dr. John Ott has described.

So whether natural sunlight or color is admitted into the body through the skin, the eyes, or by food and beverage, it does apparently promote health and well-being. The Italians have a proverb which says, "Where the sun does not enter, the doctor does."

A patient of Dr. Babbitt wrote:

Intuitively, for a long time, I have desired to expose my body to the sun, and have felt impressed to follow your directions. My husband has also taken the sun and color baths. Not having any red, yellow and blue bottles, I used panes of glass with these colors. Notwithstanding that, the effects produced upon water or food, under the action of particular stored-up rays, have astonished and surprised us. That a thing so simple should not be in daily use by all, distresses us, as we see by experiment that a glass of lukewarm water, heated by the yellow ray, is so gentle and so beneficent in its action upon the liver, the gall bladder and the bowels.

Food which has been sun-charged acquires a particular quality. It helped my digestion to become very active. Thus under the red and yellow rays I have placed bread, milk and fruit. The bread, which in ordinary state seemed heavy, became expanded and very much lighter.

As to water, since I have drunk that which has passed under the sun, I do not wish any other. Ordinary water seems hard, acrid and heavy.

If you still doubt the effects of color, Audrey Kargere, Ph.D., states that you can test these effects for yourself. She reminds us that colors are also vibrational and vary in their wavelengths, thus vary in their effect upon living matter. She suggests the following test: wrap three green tomatoes of the same size, picked at the same stage of growth, taken from the same vine. Wrap one tomato in white cloth, another in red cloth, and the third in a black cloth. Set them in the sun to ripen. When the unpicked tomatoes on the vine have ripened, unwrap your three test tomatoes. You will find that the one wrapped in the white cloth will have ripened as naturally as the ones still left on the vine.

Next, unwrap the tomato wrapped in red and cut it open. You will notice traces of black throughout the seeds and pulp, indicating that fermentation has occurred in this red-covered tomato.

Finally, unwrap the tomato wrapped in black. You will find that it has not ripened at all, and when you cut it open you will see that it has withered and decayed.

The explanation is that white is beneficial because it is a combination of all colors which it transmits; black is the absence of color; whereas the red color is stimulating and ferment-inducing.

Dr. Edwin Babbitt tells of the woman doctor serving in attendance at a Turkish bath, who believed that light-colored clothing was an excellent tonic for the skin since it is more animating than dark colors. She stated that she could tell when women had been wearing black because their skins appeared more withered. She felt any person could be cured of a cold by wearing white clothing for two days. She also recommended white underclothing because white transmits, rather than absorbs, most of the rays. This doctor believed that the skin and nerves are made more active by light, and the burden of cleansing by the lungs, liver and kidneys is lessened, thus helping the external system to become more positive.

So Dr. Kargere believes that even though we may not be aware of the effects of color around us, in our homes, surroundings or dress, it is affecting us just the same, just as those colors affected the tomatoes. Sooner or later the results will show up.

Meanwhile, the more natural foods you use, nourished by the all-colorful rays of the sun, especially the foods which are naturally and highly colored, the better for you. Thi. is a "free" source of color therapy, a healthful gift from Nature.

7. Color Therapy
for Eye Problems

Our grandparents often reported relief from eye-strain from wearing an old fashioned green eye shade. Today, color treatment is purposely being used for the eyes themselves. Gladys Mayer, in her book, *Color and Healing*, says:

The use of color naturally plays a considerable part in the treatment of the eyes. Color treatments are more potent if contrast reactions are used. For example, red and blue may be used to correct farsightedness or nearsightedness by a rhythmic succession of contrasting experiences of first one color then the other, ending with the one most needed. Blue lures the vision outward, and so helps nearsightedness; red drives it back inwardly, so can help correct farsightedness. Activity in the eye can be increased by a rhythmic and balanced alternation.

Dr. Babbitt stated, "Cold rays—blue or green—make the iris of the eyes contract and also affect the rods and cones of the eye."

Roland T. Hunt, author of many books on color therapy, reports a case of encroaching blindness due to shock, in which there was no organic eye trouble. It was remedied by changing the colors of the patient's room furnishings from orange and yellow to three shades of green. Violet light treatments were given twice a day. Partial recovery occurred in seven weeks and in seven months the sight was nearly normal.

Benedict Lust, in his book, *Natural Method of Healing Cataract*, wrote, "A form of local therapy for the cataractous eye is light treatment. Light therapy is based on the principle that light stimulates blood and lymph circulation, thus helping to eliminate congestion and to detoxicate eye tissue. Improved circulation, of course, also means improved nutrition of the entire eye. Naturally, all this will affect the lens."

Mr. Lust tells of a Dr. William Luftig, a graduate of the University of Berlin, who developed a special light technique. He combined it with other constitutional therapy and claims it has been very successful in clearing cataract cases. Even the most advanced cases, he says, responded to treatment. According to Lust:

In essence, Dr. Luftig's technique consisted in applying concentrated light on the closed eye of the patient for from two to twenty minutes, depending upon the stage of the cataract. The light source was placed one and a half yards away from the patient and the intensity of the light regulated by adjusting the focus of the light rays. If there is a hypersensitivity to light, the light rays are adjusted so that their concentration is less intense at the beginning of the treatment. Blue light may also be used for its soothing effect.

Sometimes other colors are combined to increase the response. What colors are used depends upon the individual case. Red light, for instance, has a greater stimulating effect and increases circulation. Yellow light, too, has a stimulating effect. Green light has normalizing and antiseptic qualities. In applying color therapy, the room is usually darkened to increase the response and rule out the influence of daylight.

The duration of each treatment was from five to twenty minutes, again depending upon the condition of the cataract. Usually, from twelve to twenty-four local light applications were necessary to complete the treatments.

Dr. Luftig vouches for the complete safety of the treatment, having practiced it on himself for over a year without any adverse effects. He has since tried it on innumerable patients with beneficial results. Furthermore, only a slight intensity of light is utilized. This is entirely in keeping with Arndt's famous law of physiology which says that *mild stimuli will excite physiological action, moderate ones will favor it, but strong ones will retard the action or abolish it altogether.*

An eye specialist in England has been using controlled color therapy for eye conditions for many years. R. Brooks Simpkins, author of a book, *Oculopathy*, written for professionals, as well as another book for the layman, *Visible Ray Therapy for the Eyes*, tells of exciting discoveries of the effect of color therapy on eye problems. He writes:

Glasses limit the field of vision, in conformity with the dimensions of the lenses . . . and the light rays attempting entry into the eye. Due to these restrictions the peripheral, and approximately peripheral primary rotary impulse nerve endings of the retinae, are not activated so that the external muscles of the eyes are no longer able to contract and expand. Inasmuch as any muscle is not habitually being fully contracted to expand in a normal manner, it loses tone, and such loss of tone in the six external muscles of each eye results in corresponding weakening of the coordinated muscular balance which enables motility of precise binoculation [use of both eyes].

Herein, undoubtedly, is one of the reasons why wearers of spectacles require periodic increase in the strength of their lenses, whether convex or concave, while the effect of cylindrical lenses, prescribed for astigmatism, I have found to be even more weakening, and very disturbing to the normal activity of the visual process in toto. I have found that only in very exceptional cases is astigmatism congenital in origin and becomes more marked as the infantile eye develops into the adult eye.

Frequently, immediately after an application of both energizing and sedative color rays to the eyes, the degree of astigmatism is reduced or eliminated, and the curvature of the corneal margin is found to be normal. One treatment is not, of course, sufficient to eliminate permanent astigmatical conditions, but repeated treatments are invaluable in permitting elimination of cylindrical lenses from the glasses of patients, even of middle age. This elimination is helpful to the nervous system, and often produces an unwanted sense of visual comfort.

Visible ray therapy (the use of color) gives suitable electric stimulation to the motor nerves of the eye and to the complicated visual processes generally, while instrumentally guided exercises strengthen and coordinate the complicated muscular activity for both distance and near vision.

My own case records provide substantial and extensive evidence that in the eyes of otherwise healthy adult people, senile cataract can largely be prevented from developing, and that different stages of development of this feared, and rather widespread, disease can be arrested and dispersed, and the transparency of the crystalline lens restored.

I have found that the use at home of a cheap stereoscope such as that primarily designed for the young, benefits the eyes of the middle aged and even of elderly patients who can be induced to do the exercises, and that such stereoscopic exercises help to prevent senile cataract, and to disperse it after it develops.

Mr. Simpkins treats the eyes of his patients by means of a "Fixoscope," a specially constructed lighted box-like instrument, into which the patient looks at the light through color filters. He issues this warning: "It must be remembered that in the hands of the unskilled the projection of the separated visible rays of the spectrum can be dangerous to the eyes. The energy of the projector lamps and the period of the exposure must be carefully regulated."

Mr. Simpkins begins treatment by preventing daylight from entering the room in which the color therapy is to be used for the eyes. This is done so that outside light does not dilute the color. The room, he says, should be almost dark. The Fixoscope is placed on the table so that the patient can sit in a chair and lean comfortably forward to look into the apertures, one for each eye; the distance from the 12-volt, 12-watt light bulb is approximately six inches. Although different lengths of time are allowed for treating various eye disabilities, including glaucoma, cataract, near and far sightedness, generally the same colors are used in specific alternating order. People who travel to England for these treatments and must stay in a hotel receive two treatments daily, five days a week and remain for one, two or three weeks as their needs require. For early cataract treatment, two weeks have proved sufficient, according to Simpkins; in more advanced cases, treatment is resumed after a rest of two or three months.

Patients who do not come far may receive one treatment daily for five days of each week (the weekend rest seems helpful). Here is the Simpkins schedule for a general tonic to the eyes as

well as stimulations to the intracranial processes
of vision:

The eyes are placed six inches away from a regular
12-volt 12-watt lamp bulb (not fluorescent but incandescent). Color filters are placed between the eyes
and the light. Treatments are twenty-five minutes
long as follows:

(a) Ten minutes red, ten minutes green, five minutes
blue in this sequence, or,
(b) Ten minutes orange, ten minutes green, five
minutes blue, or,
(c) Five minutes red, five minutes green, five minutes
orange or yellow, five minutes green, five minutes blue.

Mr. Simpkins explains that blue has a sedative
effect on the eyes, and for that reason he always
ends with that color. The red ray is used to stimulate, the green to relieve congestion. He adds,
"After a number of primary treatments using
chiefly the red, green and blue rays, we employ
the energizing orange and yellow rays, both for
alternating monocular and binocular stimulation
of the coordination of the retinal processes with
the visual centres of the brain, and for stimulating . . . the dilation and contraction of the pupils.
The stimulation of the yellow ray has health giving properties; the orange rays are very stimulating."

Mr. Simpkins states that he does not use the
red ray for anyone who has previously suffered a
stroke. However, red is used freely for all others,
due to its good effect in eye stimulation. The
change from red to green for the eyes, apparently,
acts and feels something like the application of

hot and cold compresses. In addition to benefitting the eyes, according to Mr. Simpkins, "The central and the sympathetic nervous systems also benefit. Even hearing and brain function have been found to improve in some cases."

Before Mr. Simpkins perfected his Fixoscope, he contrived a home-made instrument which was nothing more than two 2.5-volt flashlights, each placed behind small framed colored gelatine slides, and placed at a range of six inches from the eyes. This is worth remembering, since unfortunately, but not unexpectedly, Fixoscopes may not be imported into the United States. In explaining how color therapy affects eye problems, including cataracts and glaucoma, Mr. Simpkins writes:

We are all familiar with the properties of turpentine for thinning down paint which is too thick. The correct wavelength of green has a similar effect for congestive conditions in the eye, particularly in glaucoma. In all cases of glaucoma the green rays are of outstanding importance; the raised intra-ocular pressure usually goes down after a ten minute exposure. . . . Such persons are given an intensified treatment in the form of two treatments daily, two times a week. The green rays are also used for dispersing cataractous conditions of the crystalline lens and for cloudy and "frosted" corneal surfaces from previous ulceration. Color treatment is also useful for astigmatism and near and far-sightedness.

These visible rays give us a remedial therapy which no other method can be expected to achieve, even in many patients who had previously been told that nothing could be done for their eyes. . . . During the last quarter of a century large numbers of people have been astonished at the improvement after a single treatment.

Mr. Simpkins summarizes his use of color therapy for eyes as well as other parts of the body. He says, "Research has discovered that wave bands of color of the visible spectrum have individual and potent energic and medicinal properties which provide a natural medicine for the eyes and vision. A reaction of the retina to color also produces a vital effect upon the entire nervous system.

"The remedial effects of color may, in the not very distant future, well be employed for other organs and illnesses of the body generally, instead of drugs and chemicals."

8. How to Apply
Color Therapy

There are various methods of using color for health.

R. B. Amber believes that the best method of all is a short-time exposure of the body to the sun with as much skin bared as possible. Since the sun contains the entire color spectrum, the supposition is that the body will extract and absorb the color or colors needed, rejecting those which are not necessary. Heat and color should not be confused, according to Mr. Amber and other color experts. It is color, not heat, which supplies color healing; heat is incidental to this type of therapy.

If the sun is not available, then other methods of color treatment may be used.

Because color therapy is as old as the history of disease itself, many simple methods of color therapy have evolved. In the middle ages, colored cloth was used to treat disease. In early medicine, color and light were used, often by employing jewels and colored glass as mediums of color.

Many cures were attributed in early centuries to stained glass church windows, containing much red, purple, green and yellow, through which the sun streamed upon the ill and infirm. The bene-

ficial effects may of course have been enhanced
by prayer and music (sound therapy)*.

One example of combining color and music
therapies has been noted today in the rehabilitation of inmates in prisons and asylums. First,
working with color in painting was tried. Prisoners
were given a paint brush, colors and the encour-
agement to start painting. Men without roots
seemed to find new hope and self-respect when
given color to work with. The doctors studied the
prisoners' creations and found them helpful in
diagnosis. They learned that excessive brightness
spells hostility; deep overtones mean depression.
Since then, Vacaville State Prison in California
has produced eight major art shows, attracting
8,000 visitors. Four hundred fifty paintings have
sold for a total of $15,750.00. Best of all, however,
Dr. William C. Keating, Jr., the warden and a
Menninger Clinic trained psychiatrist, says, "Our
emphasis on art has definitely helped the inmates
to be better men." This experiment was followed
by a new use of color, according to an *Associated
Press* report in the *Los Angeles Times*, December
3, 1948:

Into the darkened wards of asylums for the insane
has come a new art form, but its discoverers didn't
know quite what to do with it. It is called *Auroratone*
and the man guiding its development is Cecil Stokes,
an Englishman.

Auroratone is a process for translating music into
color. Essentially, it is a motion picture. The theater
lights are dimmed. You hear familiar music and on
the screen flashes a series of color patterns, constantly shifting prismatic tones in every hue of the rain-

---

* Linda Clark: *Help Yourself to Health*. Pyramid Publications,
New York, 1972

bow, subtly changing with the mood of the music. Depending on the music, the effect can be relaxation, mental stimulation or emotional disturbance.

The principle is simple. The musical vibrations register on a sensitized emulsion photographed by a color movie camera. Each note creates a different color pattern in the emulsion. The color movie of these shifting changes is synchronized with the music.

Captain Herbert E. Rubin of Crile General Hospital reported in the *Journal of Clinical Psychology*, October 1946 that physical relaxation appeared to spread over the patients during the course of the film showing. Stereotyped motor phenomena such as wringing of hands, striking of parts of the body, and tics, became less intense or disappeared.

Six musical films were used in this study at Crile General Hospital. They were *Clair de Lune*, played by André Kostelanetz and his orchestra; *Going My Way*, sung by Bing Crosby accompanied at the organ by Lt. Col. Edward Unstedter, AAF; *The Lost Chord*, an organ solo; *Home On The Range*, sung by Crosby with organ accompaniment; *I Dream of Jeanie With the Light Brown Hair*, an organ solo, and Schubert's *Ave Maria*, sung by Crosby with organ accompaniment.

Most patients, according to Rubin, became more accessible immediately following exposure to the films. Those whose speech was previously blocked or retarded spoke more freely.

Dr. Carl D. Thomas, principal of Juvenile Hall in Los Angeles, has experimented with the effect of these films on juvenile delinquents. One of the children, after an *Auroratone* showing, wrote his parents, "I think God must have painted those pictures." Another confided to Dr. Thomas, "I cried for my mother during *Ave Maria*, and once I thought I saw her face in one of the color shapes."

Prints of *Auroratone films* are loaned to various military camps and hospitals for experimental purposes.

WHERE CAN YOU FIND COLOR
THERAPY EQUIPMENT?

We have now learned of several direct ways of using color therapy: on the skin, through the eyes, and by taking naturally colored foods and beverages, or even solarized, colored water. Of course, there are indirect methods of using color: in the clothes you choose, as well as the interior decoration of your own home. Unfortunately the latter may not appeal to all members of the family. One may need, or like, one color, whereas another person may need or prefer another color.

From this point forward, I wish I could tell you where to find a color therapist or where to buy color equipment for self-help purposes. Neither is allowed in this country, and I do not know of any sources of such equipment in any other countries either. If they do exist, no doubt these products would be denied entry.

In the future, we can hope that the time will come when we may have freedom of choice of our own natural health remedies, at which time both equipment and exact directions for its use will be readily available. Meanwhile you will have to improvise. You can read between the lines in the information I impart to you in this book, noting what doctors and therapists *used* to do, and perhaps adapting their methods to your own needs. I can give you a few hints, only, but you will have to put on your thinking cap and use your own ingenuity to put this reported information into practice for yourself.

EARLY METHODS OF COLOR THERAPY

The healing effect of the early stained glass windows in churches did not go unnoticed. The discovery led color therapists of that time, many of whom were physicians, to employ similar methods. As you read of Edwin D. Babbitt, M.D., and his methods used in the last century, you will agree they were no doubt copied from this idea. Colored panes of glass were placed in front of home windows and were moved to follow the sun as well as the person being treated, while he was working or resting. The colors, illuminated by sunlight, were chosen according to the individual needs (which I will explain soon). You *may* find some panes of colored glass or plastic at industrial or construction glass companies for this purpose.

Since not all colors were available in glass or plastic, some therapists have hit upon the idea of substituting colored gelatin sheets, such as those used to cover flood lights in theaters. Colored cellophane paper, though flimsy, was another possibility. The more rigid colored sheets of gelatin were used by one respected color therapist before he fled the country to avoid persecution. He made and sold a cylindrical metal lamp shade (no longer available, of course) on the lower front of which was attached a wire rack to support the chosen stiff gelatin filters, which he cut to measure approximately 10″ by 12″. The shade was placed on a gooseneck desk or floor lamp, equipped with a 100-watt incandescent bulb, and the chosen color was placed in the rack and trained on any part of the body desired.

The procedure used had been suggested by Dinshah: the person was to be treated either sitting in a chair, or reclining on a bed in a warm, dark room, with as much skin bared as possible. The color was beamed on the area needing help; the treatment usually began on the soles of the feet; the eyes remained opened. Dinshah believed that a color treatment should be taken before meals, or at least two hours afterward, three hours apart if more than one occurred in one day, and should last from minutes up to an hour, according to the needs of the individual.

Were there any side effects? Dinshah and others believed that the various colors were helpful in normalizing the body functions when directed to areas needing help. They reasoned that when the colored light played upon and around the area, the congestion was helped to be broken up. This, they felt, would release the congestion so that it could be carried away by the body's eliminative system. They were not overly concerned if some slight discomfort occurred at first while the congestion was breaking up. If, however, the discomfort became too intense, the treatment could always be promptly terminated, or a complementary color could be used to restore balance.

Dinshah believed that one should not become impatient for results in color therapy. He advised, "Give the congestion a chance to drain from the body and the vital organs a chance to regain their equilibrium."

In addition to breaking up congestion, another principle in color therapy is apparently to supply the body with the color it lacks, thus correcting its deficiency. In other words, beaming a color or colors on the body via the bare skin, appears to be a form of *feeding color to the body* through light applications rather than through food. Many therapists in the past have felt that both methods were more effective than just one used alone.

Their reasoning also assumed, and tests confirmed the supposition, that when the deficiency was corrected and the body had had its fill of a particular color, it would reject any further absorption through the light method. If, however, an imbalance of color occurred due to too much food of one color, or some abnormal cause, the supposition was that the overabundance of the color which might be causing a color imbalance could be reduced, and balance restored, by using its complementary color.

As an example, R. B. Amber believed that underweight or overweight could be due to an imbalance between red and blue in the body. He believed that underweight resulted from too much red, overweight from too much blue. His suggestion for correcting the imbalance was, in the case of underweight, to increase the intake of blue foods and to sip solarized "blue water" daily. For overweights, the correction was just the opposite: he suggested that they eat more red foods and sip red solarized water daily.

In addition to color applications via the skin, still another method is employed by a therapist, a physician, now retired and living in another country: eyeglasses into which different colors of glass could be inserted. The patient would don the spectacles with the chosen color, sit for twenty minutes at least three feet away from and facing a lamp holding a 60–100-watt bulb.

Most color therapists were explicit about the

hues they used. They chose colors according to certain, exact frequencies. Since the average person may not, at least at the present time, find these exact hues, using primary colors straight, or combining available colors to produce other needed colors could be considered satisfactory. There are, however, two types of primary colors: primary colors for pigment (as found in paints) and primary colors used with light. Mixing pigment colors, as in painting, does not give the same results as mixing colors for use with light. The primary colors for pigments are red, yellow and blue. When mixed together in certain proportions, they produce black, or absence of color.

Light primary colors, according to Newton, as well as to more recent investigators, are red, green and blue-violet. When they are mixed, they produce white light. Combining the following colors, usually available in glass or gelatine filters, produced other desired colors, perhaps otherwise unavailable.

COLOR COMBINATIONS FOR EXPERIMENTATION

red and yellow	make orange
blue and violet	make indigo
yellow and green	make lemon
green and blue	make turquoise
red and violet	make magenta (although magenta in the original form is considered preferable)
magenta and red	make scarlet
blue and red	make purple
yellow and blue	make green

COMPLEMENTARY COLORS

Pigment colors
red .... green
yellow .... violet
blue .... orange
Light Colors (according to Dinshah)
red .... turquoise
green .... magenta
violet .... lemon

Archeologists have found evidence of the use of color therapy in Egypt. There were signs that the healer would diagnose the colors in which the person was deficient, then place him in a room where color was admitted to supply restoration of the deficient color. The Egyptians also used gem or jewel therapy as well as combining color with perfumes (a different set of vibration).

The Chinese taught that colors activated man's physical, mental and spiritual being.

There are many references to color therapy in Edgar Cayce's clairvoyant readings, including the following which explain some previously unanswered questions. The readings were, of course, for different individuals with different disturbances. Nevertheless, the information is enlightening.

Example 1: In most instances where a change in vibration is needed, the projection of a green light is preferable, because green is the healing vibration. Have the light at least 37 to 38 inches from the body.

Example 2: We would use the green light or glass between the body and the ultraviolet light; one and one-half minutes over the lower cervical and upper dorsal area.

Example 3: Do rest for at least fifteen minutes under the ultraviolet light. But do always have the green light between the ultraviolet light and the body. The ultraviolet light should be at least 60 inches away from the body and *only* the Mercury light (lamp). The green light (filter) should be 8" x 10" or 12", and 12" to 14" from the body. These are the healing influences of that taken out of the infraray.

As proof of the more recent effectiveness of color for the *body* when received through the *eyes,* an *Associated Press* release reported a method of color healing for burns. This method consisted of a light-filtering green dye painted on a black and white television screen, intended to help relax the eyes during viewing. However, the inventor discovered that it also stopped the pain of burns within a half hour.

The dye, according to the news release, acts somewhat like a pair of colored sunglasses, allowing only certain rays of light to penetrate the eye (and as later realized, the body). The discovery resulted from the inventor's attempt to duplicate the light filtration capability of chlorophyl, found in nature's green plants.

Dr. Francis L. Owens, a staff member of a North Carolina hospital, found that a colored green film used over a light bulb definitely helped in the treatment of burns. He first tried it on a three-year-old child who had fallen into a bucket of boiling starch and acquired second and third degree burns. Owens said, "All pain was relieved in a half hour. The child never cried anymore and within a week all of the burned area was healed except a deeply burned spot on top of her foot. None of the burned area became infected and there was little scar tissue."

Dr. Owens also cited other cases in which the filter was used to treat burns. Pain again ceased quickly. Similar results have been documented in a New York hospital.

There are other methods of color therapy in addition to the irradiation of the body or eyes by color filters—by means of lamps. A report in the *Australian Post*, August 5, 1955, tells of the surge of interest in color therapy in New Zealand:

New Zealanders by the thousand are flocking to color therapists, seeking treatment for illness and disease. In the city of Wanhanui (population 30,000) queues have reached from the second story therapists' offices to the street. On sheep stations, wool farmers are treating their flocks with color. They even employ the color therapists to test valuable stud rams for fertility.

It is surprising that color therapy has attracted such a startling number of adherents in a country that ranks top in the world for state care of the sick and the injured. In New Zealand doctors and hospitals are virtually free of charge throughout the country. A beneficent social security system has made fear of doctors' bills a thing of the past. Even prescriptions filled at the chemist shops [drug stores] are "on the house."

Yet color therapists, who charge hard cash, cannot cope with the rush to their offices. The color therapists believe that all kinds of bacteria or diseases give off a wave length which they can pick up by the use of a pendulum—a form of dowsing or water divining. The principle theory for treatment by the colors found indicated for each individual is the claim that a germ or disease cannot live in its own wave length. The color therapists claim if a color which gives off the same wave length as the condition from which the patient may be suffering is broadcast to the patient, the germs die or the condition is eliminated and the patient gets well.

Once the therapists identify the disease, they go to work to "cure" it.

The method of color therapy most popular in New Zealand is by the use of a copper coil. *After identifying the disease the patient is suffering from through pendulum testing* of a huge range of different colored strands of silk or thread, previously correlated to match the wave length of the disease, the patient lies on a bed while a magnet coil is placed at his feet. A piece of colored silk representing the wave length of the disease is placed on the contact point on the coil.

One New Zealand veterinarian uses giant wire coils to treat flocks of sheep as they graze on the farms. Some sheep farmers have also adopted this system of curing animal diseases. Big wire coils stuck in the ground, broadcasting the correct color, are said to be "curing" sheep of intestinal complaints, sheep jaundice and other diseases.

The veterinarian began his successful color therapy practice with sheep when his own health responded to color therapy after all orthodox methods had failed.

Faber Birren, a color consultant for industry, schools and hospitals, has done long and thorough research on every aspect of color. His monumental work, *Color Psychology and Color Therapy,** contains these statements:

It is unfortunate that in America the medical profession by and large disdains the general subject of color therapy. There is the tendency to deny any and all therapeutic phenomena. This attitude is traditional with American science, for in this country

---

* New Hyde Park, N.Y. University Books, Inc., 1961

basic and theoretical science have never been greeted as enthusiastically as applied science. American medical men are presumably not interested in color. . . .

However, despite so contrary an attitude in America, it is largely meaningless and futile to deny the reality of color therapy. Visible light *does* affect the human organism. Anyone who insists otherwise is merely bespeaking prejudice and closing his mind to a great mass of reliable and competent evidence.

The foregoing should give you some suggestion of the various possibilities for the use of color therapy. You can take it from there.

The late George Starr White, M.D., said, "I could fill a big book with clinical case records to prove that this light and color system is opening up a field for giving health and contentment to countless sufferers."

Rex D. Hetherington, in his book, *Color—Its Power, Action and Therapeutic Value*, adds, "Notes from over 50,000 cases derived from forty sources and thirty years of color therapy witness the effect of color. Today we know how to separate color for special purposes and effects."

The following chapter includes descriptions of these separate colors and their uses. They have been extracted from scores of books, thousands of cases, and presented for your consideration. They represent not *claims*, but actual *reports* of what has happened as a result of color therapy. We can apply color in myriad ways to add cheer and enhance our surroundings, as well as to improve health physically and emotionally. Without color, life would be drab and dreary. With it, a sparkle is added; joy can follow.

9. Properties of
Individual Colors

RED

Red is considered a warm color, stimulating the body in a constructive manner, and has been used to disperse congestion. For anemia, beaming red toward the area behind the heart is said to raise the blood count. Red radiation to this same area on the back has also been surprisingly used for hemorrhages in the body as well as for helping to manufacture new red cells.

Investigators in color therapy believe that any area of the body which needs stimulation can benefit from beaming red upon it. Used on the soles of the feet, it has been reported to improve poor circulation; and radiated around the navel and groins, to help sluggish intestines.

In 1940 a number of studies of the effect of color were conducted in Japan and reported in international medical journals. In experiments with guinea pigs, the younger generation attained rapid growth following irradiation with red light.

Red irradiation on rabbits showed no immediate results, but the Japanese reported an unexpected, though delayed, reaction in a drop in blood pressure. "No matter whether the red ray was applied to the whole body or abdomen, it tended to lower blood pressure," the report stated.

Friedrich Ellinger in his book, *The Biologic Fundamentals of Radiation Therapy*, found that irradiation of the heads of four and five month-old blind ducklings, resulted in a better development of the sex organs than for the control group which was not irradiated. Ludwig and von Ries, noted experimenters, found that red light undoubtedly does affect the living organism; it may promote more rapid growth and weight, although, according to Ellinger, if young rats are irradiated with red *only*, they eventually die, presumably from a vitamin deficiency.

Faber Birren states, "Red light has frequently been specified for erysipelas, urticaria, scarlet fever, measles, and eczema." Kuster has employed it favorably in cases of excessive functioning of the sex organs and uterine hemorrhages. It has been found to reduce pain in post-operative incision, acute inflammation and ultraviolet burn. R. Douglas Howat* refers to its value in the treatment of lumbago, myalgia, rheumatoid arthritis, sciatica, neuritis and fractures.

Other researchers report that red, being the warmest of all colors, apparently increases circulation, vitality, energy, and warmth in the tissues. It is said to stimulate the nerves, liver; improve anemia, and red fractions in the blood. It has also been used to stimulate the various senses which include seeing, hearing, smelling and feeling, and to aid sluggish conditions as well as paralysis. As a counter-irritant, its heat has been found excel-

---

* *Elements of Chromotherapy*, London, Actinic Press, 1938

lent for contraction of muscles. Dr. Babbitt gives
a case history of rehabilitation from complete
physical exhaustion by bathing the body with red
light:

Mr. R., 45 years of age, an overtaxed and prematurely wornout businessman, became involved in finan-
cial troubles. His mind and body were continuously
on the rack; he could neither eat nor sleep normally,
and at last, complete physical exhaustion and nervous
prostration came upon him, for nature could endure
no more.

The first warning was severe pains in the back of
the head, soon followed by shortness of breath, flut-
terings of heart, compressible pulse, loss of appetite,
constipation and phosphatic urine. I determined to
try the red light treatment, especially as his prostration was unattended by any indication of morbid
irritability, and in all my experience as a physician,
I have never witnessed more remarkable beneficial
results than were at once produced by the red ray
in this case.

The very first color bath had the most encouraging
effect: it acted as a tonic upon both mind and body,
dispelled his gloomy apprehensions and gave vigor to
his physical functions. Commencing with small doses
(length of time), I gradually increased them until
assured that I had reached the most effective dose in
length of exposure. Mr. R. rapidly improved, notwithstanding his continued attention to business.
From the first he slept more refreshingly, ate with
better relish, his bowels became regular, and the
secretions of his kidneys recovered. Three weeks'
treatment sufficed, and there have been no signs of
relapse.

You have already read of the amazing results produced by the late Dr. Oscar Brunler in connection
with his medical practice of color therapy in Lon-

don. You will remember his success with the use of the red ribbon for the asthmatic child. He adds further information on the use of red:

Rheumatism is an accumulation of wastes, including uric acid. Flooding the body with red light dissolves these crystals in the joints which have resulted from malfunctioning kidneys.

Wear a red scarf around the neck for colds.

Weak or nervous children should be surrounded by red colors to make them more courageous; their nervousness will abate as red forces the body to greater activity.

Dr. Brunler also believed that red increases blood cells, as well as being bactericidal in effect, and that it should be used instead of ultraviolet for this purpose.

Dr. Brunler's reputation for success with color therapy spread far and wide in England. He said, "Although color research exists in England, Vienna, Italy, France, Switzerland, Holland, Belgium, Sweden, Japan and India, the medical profession and physicists in America have paid no attention to these researches."

The late Roland Hunt gives suggestions for methods of using general systemic red color therapy:

When taking light treatment, the patient lies flat upon a bed. The red light is projected first upon the soles of the feet.

During treatment the projections from the lamp, or sun filters, should be gradually raised from the soles of the feet to the ankles, then calves, following up to the knees, then the thighs, resting from five to ten minutes at each location.

If a specific area needs treatment, the color projections can be beamed there for approximately twenty minutes.

Treatment is finished off with green or blue light to counteract any undesirable or irritating physiological or psychological effects.

Contra-indications of Red. Too much of anything can often be disturbing. Dr. Babbitt explains instances when red can be harmful. He says, "Red is injurious when there is already too much of the red or inflammatory condition in the system, perhaps indicated by red hair, an over-red face, or feverish or excitable conditions."

Others agree that red, though indeed a tonic for those who need it, and considered helpful for rheumatism, paralysis and physical exhaustion, can be injurious for those who already have too much red, or in the case of inflammatory conditions. Redhaired people, also, according to Dr. Audrey Kargere, should use very little red. Even iron seems to be contra-indicated in inflammatory conditions, she says. The late George Starr White, M.D., wrote:

If employed to excess as to amount or time, the red light overexcites the nervous system and may produce dangerous fevers or other disorders that may prove as troublesome as the conditions we are seeking to correct. We *seldom employ red light to the exclusion of the other rays, and it should never be so employed except in extreme cases.* [Emphasis mine.]

The danger of the exclusive red light may be averted by using the light through the red glass only for a few minutes at first, taking precaution, when the system becomes too hot, to put blue glass (an antidote to red) in its place. For general cases it would be better to have a wet bandage or a blue pane of glass shining on the head and a red pane of glass

radiating the rest of the body. Infrared rays should
never be used.

Red Foods Iron and copper are present in foods
that often are known to increase vitality. They include beets (tops and roots), tomatoes, radishes,
red cabbage, watercress, spinach, black cherries,
red currants, red plums, red beans, watermelon,
grapes, whole wheat, liver and red wine.

Roland T. Hunt suggested for those who need
red, drinking several glasses of "red" solarized
water between meals. He advised that the con-
tainer should be filled with fresh water every two
days in hot weather, every ten days in winter,
before exposure to the sun.

SCARLET

Scarlet, a variation of red, is, according to these
investigators, considered a cerebral (brain) stimulant, reduces inflammation, and serves as an
arterial stimulant and kidney energizer as well as
a general healer throughout the body.

Scarlet used psychologically represents courage. On days when vitality and morale are low,
one may wear flame or scarlet red to disperse
discouragement. I can vouch for this since I have
tried it!

PINK

Pink, a pastel tint of red, according to Dr.
Brunler, affects the mind more than the body.
He warned, if you are a poor sleeper, not to

sleep under pink blankets. Use pale blue, instead, he said.

Dr. Brunler also advised not using pink for temperamental or highly excitable people. He said, "People who live on their nerves should never have pink surroundings or wall colors." On the plus side, pink is considered the color of universal healing, with a potential for raising the vibrations of the body. An exciting use of pink for rejuvenation is described in Chapter 12, Breathing Color.

ORANGE

The spectroscopic color of calcium is orange. Since calcium deficiency is now found to be so common, especially in government surveys, perhaps this explains why the color orange has proved so beneficial in so many ailments.

Orange is apparently a body normalizer; it has been used in asthmas and respiratory disorders, and no doubt due to its calcium relationship, is considered an anti-rachitic (anti-rickets). It is considered helpful for cramps and spasms, an aid to digestion and has provided relief for ulcers and improved thyroid function. Orange color also has helped to replenish depleted enthusiasm as well as depleted vitality. Some therapists have beamed orange on the spleen, heart and throat center during energy depletion. Yellow or golden orange appears to improve glossiness and softness of hair.

Dr. Oscar Brunler found that golden-orange has a powerful effect on the thyroid as well as on the liver. He felt that it releases nerve tension, increases gland activity, and makes the heartbeat stronger. In some people he found that it increased blood pressure. You may remember that it was golden-orange beamed to the group of partially intoxicated men who, as a result, refused further alcohol during the study. He radiated the livers of diabetics with golden-orange and succeeded in lowering the daily intake of insulin from 145 to 25 units. He also used golden-orange on the throat of the voiceless actress, restoring her voice within minutes.

The late Col. Dinshah P. Ghadiali, originally of India, later a resident of the United States, has written a compendium of color therapy based on his many years of research with patients from all over the world. His book, *Spectro-Chrome-Metry,* an encyclopedia in three volumes, no longer in print, contains an immense amount of information on color therapy. According to Dinshah, which he was called, as mentioned earlier, the color orange stimulates and helps rebuild the lungs, aids bronchitis, activates the thyroid, and depresses the parathyroid glands. It aids the digestion by relieving gas, brings relief in intestinal cramps and spastic and sluggish colon and intestines.

Dinshah also claims orange increases all kinds of eliminative discharges including menstrual craps and deficient flow, as well as acting as a stimulant for breast milk in infant feeding. Orange has also been used to bring boils, carbuncles and abscesses to a head.

Because of its affinity for calcium, Dinshah considers orange rays superior to cod liver oil for treating rickets. Due to its calcium qualities, it has been used for soft bones, soft teeth, tuberculosis and poor posture. Dinshah maintains that it relieves hiccoughs.

In general, Dinshah believes that orange is closely related to the following physiological functions: liver, spleen, stomach, pancreas, kidney, bladder, lungs and respiratory system, and to such ailments as epilepsy, asthma, stomach complaints, kidney stones and gravel, gallstones, gout, rheumatism and arthritis.

His findings indicate that yellow eyes as well as blue fingernails point to a deficiency of both red and yellow (which combined make orange), and psychological reactions of such a deficiency have been noted as depression, melancholia, hyperirritability and chronic fear. Dinshah used the orange color filter on the affected part of the body, including the soles of the feet, legs and the area slightly below the navel.

The late Roland Hunt suggested in addition to orange light therapy, that orange-irradiated water be taken between meals.

Various therapists have reported good results from these color techniques practiced daily, every three days, or periodically as desired and according to individual needs and tolerance. They agree that it may or may not take many weeks or even months before the various conditions are corrected.

Roland Hunt cites a case history: One patient suffered from kidney inflammation for seven years. He was advised to use orange light directed on the kidney area and to drink orange-irradiated water. On the third day he passed a large amount of small gravel and has been free of kidney pains ever since.

Mr. Hunt also believed that a wet cough, which is accompanied by phlegm, is helped by orange light as well as drinking orange-irradiated water. He recommended the use of the light twice in the morning and once in the evening to arrest the condition and expel the phlegm. He believed that this intensive treatment might relieve the condition within two weeks.

My friend Joanna related an experience which is an excellent example of the effects of orange. She had been extremely ill and her recovery began the day a friend of hers came to visit her wearing a jacket made of bright, vivid red, yellow and orange. She said afterwards, "Those colors gave me a tremendous lift. I couldn't take my eyes off of them. It was my first step toward more energy and subsequent recovery."

Orange Foods. Carrots, sweet potatoes, pumpkins, oranges and tangerines, squash, peaches, apricots, canteloupe, mangoes, persimmons, papaya, eggs and dairy products, all provide orange.

YELLOW

Yellow was considered by Dinshah a motor (muscle) stimulant and a nerve builder par excellence. It has been found to act as a laxative, increase flow of bile, increase stomach and intestinal activity and reduce swelling. Golden yellow appears to be a lubricant and healer. In the deep amber tones it has been found helpful for constipation and some forms of arthritis.

According to Dinshah, yellow activates all of the body functions, except the spleen, which is depressed by it. It helps build nerves and muscles, stimulates the heart for better circulation, stimulates the liver and gall bladder, helps eliminate intestinal parasites, aids indigestion and constipation. Dinshah indicated that yellow has helped diabetes, stimulated the pancreas, loosened calcium deposits in neuritis and arthritis, and stimulated eyes and ears. It also improved skin texture, aided pore cleansing and the healing of scars and blemishes.

Dr. Oscar Brunler stated that yellow carries a negative charge. Dinshah added that, even though you might be unaware of parasites, by beaming yellow on the abdominal area, if they are there, the parasites cannot stand the color and will move on. He also stated that tonating with yellow light has stimulated the gastric juices including bile, hydrochloric acid and pepsin, and thus has aided indigestion.

Roland Hunt points out that yellow in the orange range is warming; in the pure tones is cooling and astringent. Hunt suggests the exposure to yellow twice daily, plus a glass of yellow-irradiated water taken frequently between meals. He warns that complete correction of chronic cases may take two months.

Dr. Babbitt prescribed two-to-four tablespoons of yellow-charged water before each meal, or even every hour, for those suffering with severe constipation. He writes:

Yellow-charged water is one of the most important of medicines for nerve animation. It also animates the kidneys, liver, and has cured cases of chronic constipation after the best known drugs had been tried in vain.

A New York millionaire, whose bowels would not move excepting by the aid of medicines, found the yellow-charged water answered every purpose. It gave him such a cheerful feeling that he said it was worth $1000. In a few cases this water does not act as a laxative, but this is attributable to a more or less inflammable condition of the stomach. In this case, take the blue-charged water on retiring for several nights or focus the yellow lens over the liver and bowels.

A woman wrote Dr. Babbitt as follows:

I have been using the water charged in the yellow-orange glass with wonderful, I think marvelous, effect. Though the sun did not shine for three weeks when I first received it, I kept the yellow glass in the window where it could catch every chance ray, taking a sip or two of the water every hour, until now I am as regular as need be. You can imagine how delighted and grateful I am when you know it is over eight years since I had a natural movement.

Dr. Babbitt warns that yellow can be injurious and over-exciting to a system already active and irritable. In fevers, acute inflammation, delirium, diarrhea, neuralgia and palpitation of the heart or over-excitement of any kind, it is not indicated, he says.

Dr. Kargere agrees with other researchers that yellow is especially good for nerves, can act as a purgative and stimulates the kidneys. It has caused the skin to perspire and has an affinity for the liver and bile as well as stimulating the brain. She tells of the medical experiment showing the healing effects of yellow light: "There was a case of bronchial irritation which, when treated with a yellow light over the chest, was able to show some results within a minute. The condition cleared up completely with treatment of yellow applied for twenty minutes daily for several days."

On the other hand, Dr. Kargere also warns that yellow can overstimulate nervous conditions such as insomnia, diarrhea and delirium. Nerves of the insane are irritated by yellow. Dr. Kargere adds, "Even so mild a substance as coffee, with its yellow-brown radiations, creates a tendency toward wakefulness. Those who wish to escape some of the worst effects of coffee should not let it steep more than five or ten minutes, at which time the grounds should be removed to prevent the tannin from escaping into the liquid. The tannin is the astringent principle in coffee, whereas coffee alone has a laxative and diuretic effect."

Yellow may stimulate the intellect, providing it is of a light, clear tone. If you are suffering from mental confusion, try writing on clear yellow paper.

In a dark, sunless room, yellow provides a feeling of cheer.

Yellow Foods. These include parsnips, yellow corn, yellow sweet potatoes, bananas, banana squash, pineapples, lemons, grapefruit, honeydew melons, butter, eggs, yellow cheese, and most yellow-skinned fruits and vegetables.

LEMON-YELLOW

Lemon-yellow is contained in gold, iodine, iron, phosphorus, silver and sulphur. Colorwise, it includes some green which gives it slightly different qualities than orange-yellow or golden-yellow.

Lemon-yellow has been found to be a blood purifier and apparently loosens and eliminates mucus throughout the entire body, thus has been effective in relieving colds. This may explain why the lemon fruit is so effective in these afflictions.

Dinshah stated that lemon-yellow is an antacid, a laxative, a bone builder, an expectorant, a cerebral stimulant, anti-scurvy (as we know the lemon fruit is), activates the thymus gland, is useful for sluggish liver, and helps dullness of memory.

GREEN

Dr. Oscar Brunler found that green affects the whole system, and is particularly beneficial for the sympathetic nervous system, as well as helpful in increasing vitality. Green has also been used for kidneys and liver, which must work hard to counteract polluted air, food and water. It is considered useful for promoting general healing, restoration and balance.

Dinshah considered green the master healer. He believed that if you do not know what color to use, you will always be right with green. He claimed that it accomplishes the following: acts as a detergent, stimulates the pituitary (which in turn stimulates the other glands); dissolves blood clots; builds muscles, tissues and skin; breaks up congestions and hardened cell masses; eliminates germs and viruses and toxic waste matter, including open sores; increases or decreases blood pressure by affecting it through the liver. He believed that too little green may create gall bladder problems including stones.

Dr. Babbitt stated that he has successfully treated ulcers with green. Roland Hunt recommended body exposure to the green ray and drinking green irradiated water, one-half glass at half-hour intervals between meals.

Green eyeshades worn ten to thirty minutes

daily were found by several investigators to be helpful to the optic nerve. However, excessive use may cause neuralgic headaches.

Dr. Babbitt states that green is a quieting color if it is not too dark a green. Grass green—nature's leaf green—is a guide to the correct shade, he says.

Green Foods. Since green occurs in so many vegetables, eating them raw as well as cooked is an excellent way to get the health-giving chlorophyl into the body. Raw green salads, green cabbage, green asparagus, green celery, green peppers, as well as green peas, string beans and spinach are just a few possibilities.

Yellow-green. This combination of colors has been considered a help for the regeneration of the body, and a factor in youthfulness as well as in loss of enthusiasm.

Blue-green. You will find this color to be calming, soothing; it also is considered helpful in allaying fevers and inflammation, as well as in strengthening organs with lowered tone due to stress.

TURQUOISE

Turquoise is made by combining blue and green. Dinshah considers turquoise an excellent tranquilizer, as well as being cooling and relaxing. He claims it aids headaches and swelling, decreases brain activity, is a skin builder, and helps nutrition and repair.

Turquoise, in his opinion, is excellent for the

skin, not only for treating burns; sunburn and relieving itching, but for imparting beauty to the
skin itself.

I have seen pictures of Dinshah, and his skin
even at an advanced age appeared flawless. He
gave full credit to the use of turquoise irradiated
on his skin at least twice weekly. He believed that
beauty salons should radiate a turquoise light for
a short time on the skin of every patron.

BLUE

Blue is apparently a very important color. It is
the opposite, and thus an antidote, of red, due to
its cooling qualities. It has been used for fevers,
as a depressant for motor nerves, fast pulse, pain,
reducing temperatures, as a pulmonary sedative,
and as an aid in combatting infection or inflammation. It has encouraged relaxation.

Light blue has reduced many cases of high blood
pressure. The effects have been maintained after
treatment.

According to Dr. Ernest Stevens, blue has been
used to calm, subdue, soothe and heal physical
and mental agitation.

Dr. Babbitt writes, "When violent and maniacal
patients were placed in rooms where the red ray
dominated, they became worse and all their violent
symptoms were aggravated. If these patients were
removed to a room where the blue ray predom-
inated, they became calm and quiet."

Dr. Babbitt says, "Blue is also one of the greatest
antiseptics in the world."

He claims it can stop bleeding of lungs, decrease

fevers, cure sore throats, laryngitis, hoarseness, dysentery, jaundice, cuts, burns, bruises, female diseases and acute rheumatism.

Faber Birren says, "Blue has been prescribed to cure 'thumping' headaches, high blood pressure of nervous origin, and intractable insomnia. Whether its action is direct or indirect (through the eye and emotions) matters little.

"In the Japanese studies with animals, under blue light, blood pressure dropped immediately but was followed by a pronounced rise . . . using blue dye (to absorb red light), healing of wounds was quickened."

Dr. Oscar Brunler makes some interesting comments about blue: "Royal blue is not good for sitting rooms, since it is too silencing on conversation." He adds, "However, if you are a poor sleeper, visualize blue all around you. (If you want to stay awake, visualize red). Elderly people should be in a blue rather than a pink room. All high blood pressure people should wear blue pajamas to reduce excitability and nerve tension."

In this connection it is interesting to note that blue night lights are often installed in Pullman sleepers and in some hotel rooms. A blue window shade has been found to promote daytime relaxation.

Dr. Brunler continues, "Researchers in Vienna discovered in 1930 that a shade of blue slightly lighter than royal blue, corresponds to the vibrations of healthy nerve tissue. Colitis, dysentery, diarrhea, have disappeared after drinking blue solarized water."

Dr. Babbitt supplies many case histories of the effect of blue. Here are some examples:

Mr. T., aged 35. In consequence of long continued excessive physical and mental exertion, his nervous system was entirely disordered; the derangement manifested itself in nervousness, and irritability; he could not sleep at night; he was disturbed by frightful dreams; his appetite was variable, sometimes ravenous, at others, the very sight of food was an annoyance; his bowels varied, too, at times constipated, at others lax; he had frequent pains in his head, the least excitement unnerved him, and he was inclined to extreme despondency. His irritability forbade red light, so I determined to administer blue light. The beneficial results were immediate; his entire system improved rapidly; five blue color radiation baths actually restored a healthy tone to his nervous system, and he has since experienced not a single symptom of nervousness, though his life is one of constant physical and mental activity.

Here is a statement made by a woman to Dr. Babbitt: *

"Having been an invalid for nearly three years, and for the last half of that time confined entirely to my rooms on one floor, I became so reduced in vitality by the long confinement, and my nervous system seemed so completely broken down, that all tonics lost their effects. Sleep at nights could only be obtained by the use of opiates. Appetite, of course, was non-existent, and scarcely a vestige of color remained either in my lips, face or hands. As a last resort I was placed, by my doctor, about the 19th of January, 1894, under the influence of the blue glass rays. Two large panes of the glass, each 36 inches long by 16 inches wide, were placed in the upper part of a sunny window in my parlor, a window with a south exposure, and as the blue sunlight streamed into the

* In quoting from Dr. Babbitt's book, I have, without changing the meaning, updated his language in a few cases. Cf. Babbitt, *The Principles of Light & Color*, pp. 311-312

room, I sat in it continuously. I was also advised by
my doctor to make a regular sunbath of it; at least,
to let the blue rays fall directly on the bare spine for
about 20 or 30 minutes at a time, morning and after-
noon; but the effects of it were too strong for me to
bear. As I was progressing very favorably, by merely
sitting in it in my ordinary dress, that was considered
sufficient.

"In two or three weeks the change began to be very
perceptible. The color began returning to my face,
lips and hands, my nights became better, my appetite
more natural, and my strength and vitality began to
return, while my whole nervous system was most de-
cidedly strengthened and soothed.

"In about six weeks I was allowed to try going up
and down a few stairs at a time, being able to test
in that way how my strength was returning. By the
middle of April, when the spring was sufficiently advanced to make it prudent for me to try walking
outside, I was able to do so.

"The experiment was a fair one by the stoppage of
all tonics, etc., as soon as the glass was placed in the
window, allowing me to depend solely on the efficacy
of the blue light."

Dr. Babbitt adds, "In the above case the lady had
a large mass of blue glass sufficiently great to
cover almost, if not entirely, the whole of her
body. Apparently it was too exciting for so sensitive a person in her depleted condition. A proper
(lighter) tint of blue would not have been 'too
strong' on the bare skin."

A letter written to Dr. Babbitt, reads: "Dear Sir:
The blue lens I got from you last spring (1879)
has done me incalculable good in quieting my over-
excited nervous system, producing sleep when
every other sedative either failed or left results
more to be deplored than insomnia itself. Signed,
Rev. Joseph Waite, Malton, Ontario."

Dr. Babbitt reports several cases of baldness cured by blue light. One woman who had lost all of her hair acquired a healthy head of hair due to exposure to blue light, he says.

Dr. Kargere states that violet, indigo and blue, which are astringent, are also soothing and anti-inflammatory. She reports the good effects of blue light treatment which has reversed cerebro-spinal meningitis, neuralgic headache, general nervousness, sunstroke, sciatica, nervous irritability as well as mental emotional disturbance. She cites the case of an elderly woman who had not been free of pain for a single day for eleven years. Her left leg, knee, ankle and foot were swollen to double their size. Three panes of blue glass were inserted in the window and in two hours time, the purplish color, pain and soreness disappeared. However, at night, at first, the pain returned. When the daily blue light treatment was continued, the swelling and soreness disappeared; the woman was able to walk around the house and, with continued treatment, her leg was restored to normal. Dr. Kargere also cited a case of violent hemorrhage of the lungs which was reversed by blue light treatment.

Dr. Babbitt advises that in all cold, pale, dormant conditions, such as paralysis, constipation, chronic rehumatism, as well as melancholia and depression, blue is *contra-indicated*. However, in extreme nervous tension, he considers a pure blue light bath by sun or lamp for two hours most effective. Dr. Babbitt also considers blue-irradiated water extremely helpful for disturbances already mentioned.

Those who may still remain skeptical of the

whole idea might be interested in the following report on blue light treatment which appeared in the *Philadelphia Inquirer*, May 8, 1964, as reported by staff reporter Donald C. Drake:

British and European doctors have been using the strange "blue light" treatment since it was discovered accidentally in 1958, but until just recently American pediatricians have steadfastly resisted it. Strange as it sounds, this procedure, using simple blue light —not ultraviolet—does seem to be working, and the technique is slowly being adopted by some Philadelphia institutions, notably Temple University Hospital.

With probably the largest controlled study in the area, Dr. Thomas R. S. Sission, associate professor of pediatrics at Temple, reports that the blue light has been highly effective, 150 cases since it was first used in February, 1958. The blue light therapy apparently works by breaking down bilirubin as it passes through the small blood vessels close to the surface of the skin where the blue light can get through.

Bilirubin is a yellowish substance formed when the body for one reason or another breaks down hemoglobin, the red cell material that transports oxygen. If bilirubin climbs too high in infants who have livers too immature to handle the excess, brain damage and cerebral palsy can result. The most common sign is jaundice. Most susceptible are so-called RH or ABO babies, infants whose blood is incompatible with the mothers', resulting in blood cell damage and bilirubin buildup.

Dr. Sission estimated that thirty percent of the babies at Temple have high bilirubin levels; though not all of the levels are so high as to require the treatment with the blue lights. In the past, the only treatment for high bilirubin babies was total blood transfusion in which all the blood is taken out of the baby and replaced. Not only is this time-consuming and costly, it has some dangers. One doctor reports a mortality of one to four percent, but another doctor said properly done in selected cases there is practically no mortality.

In any case, the blue light shined on babies for seventy-two hours at Temple has cut the need for cross transfusions to practically zero in ABO babies. In RH babies, it has sharply reduced the number of transfusions needed.

Dr. Thomas R. Boggs, in charge of the nursery at Pennsylvania Hospital, is one of the stronger skeptics in Philadelphia, but even he says the system looks very promising. He added, however, that he would like to see more controlled studies to find out what possible long-term diverse effects, if any—such as biochemical abnormalities—might occur before using it extensively himself.

At Hahnemann Medical College and Hospital, blue light therapy is used on all premature infants and it has resulted in a marked reduction in bilirubin levels and blood transfusions, reports Dr. Gerald Fendrick, in charge of the nursery. The Albert Einstein Medical Center also is using the system with good results, according to a report by Dr. L. Roy Newman.

The system was accidentally discovered in 1958 by an English physician who noticed that children lying in bassinets near the window where blue light filtered in were less likely to develop blood problems than those in darker corners of the nursery.

Blue Foods. These include blueberries, blue plums and prunes, grapes and others.

INDIGO

Indigo is a combination of deep blue and violet. Roland Hunt found it useful in any areas in the body needing purifying, including the blood, as well as for eye inflammation and ear problems, including deafness. For fevers connected with the lymph glands, he reported that it has been beamed at the groins, and under the armpits. Indigo is a powerful color and should be used sparingly, he noted.

Dinshah found that indigo gives relief from swellings and from extreme pain.

According to Dinshah, indigo has been found to stimulate the parathyroids, depress the thyroid, purify the blood stream, build phagocytes in the spleen, treat acute bronchitis, convulsions, nervous ailments, lung and nasal disturbances, tonsillitis and whooping cough. He also found it to be a sedative, and helpful for hemorrhages, including internal bleeding and nose bleeds. He considered indigo an astringent for tightening and toning muscles, nerves and skin. He further found it helpful for curing dysentery and mucous colitis, as well as for destroying harmful micro-organisms.

Indigo has been found to filter out radiation. Indigo solarized water, and foods in the blue and violet groups (blueberries, blue plums, blue grapes) have been used for indigo color therapy purposes.

VIOLET

Violet has been found to stimulate the spleen and the building of white blood cells; has regulated tension of blood vessels and lowering high blood pressure.

According to Dinshah, violet stimulates the spleen, depresses lymph and motor nerves. It helps to maintain the potassium-sodium balance in the body. Violet is also used for bladder trouble, concussion, cramps, epilepsy, kidneys (overactive), neuralgia, nervous and mental disorders, rheumatism, sciatica, scalp and skin disorders.

He warns, "DO NOT USE AN ULTRAVIOLET LAMP."

Dinshah also stated that violet depresses all overactive conditions of glands and organs, including lymphatic glands. Violet is also said to assist the appetite in reducing overweight; acts as a heart depressant; is relaxing and soothing to nerves and the muscles controlling the heart. It is considered an excellent soothing agent for serious mental conditions, overexcitement and overstimulation. It has apparently helped diarrhea and is considered a remedy par excellence for inducing deep, relaxed sleep.

Roland Hunt told of a case history of a businessman who, though he did not believe in color therapy, decided he would try violet for a severe neuralgic headache. He sat under the irradiation of a blue-violet glass for thirty minutes and apparently was entirely relieved of pain.

Hunt added that violet, in the shade of Parma violets, is said to be a general decongestant for the entire body. It is considered very potent. It is also found helpful for the adrenal glands.

PURPLE

Purple, a deeper shade, seems to aid vascular dilation of blood vessels working through the lymphatics.

Dinshah stated that purple has stimulated activity in the veins, depressed kidney action, induced sleep, lowered body temperature. He said that beaming purple on the heart region during throbbing or palpitations, would bring relief within minutes.

Dr. Babbitt considered purple-charged water excellent for indigestion.

Purple Foods. Foods chosen from both blue and purple groups fit into the category of violet: purple broccoli and red cabbage, beet tops, purple grapes, blackberries, blueberries and similar foods.

MAGENTA

Magenta is produced by combining red and violet. Dinshah was very enthusiastic about magenta. He found that it should be used in *all* heart disorders. He also found it helpful for bronchial ailments and as an aid in dissolving kidney stones. It has served as a general stimulant throughout the body. He discovered that it was a diuretic, helped the circulatory system, stimulated the adrenals, energized the heart, and provided emotional equilibrium.

Dinshah considered magenta, though little known and used, a most important color for healing. He said if one didn't know whether the blood pressure was too high or too low, magenta raised or lowered it automatically as needed. Similarly he claimed it stimulated or depressed the veins and arteries. He felt that nothing could be as beneficial in all forms of heart conditions as magenta, and has used it around the heart and kidney areas with excellent success.

Other properties of these colors, and of black and white which are not included in this chapter, will be found in Chapter 11, "Auras."

10. Gem Therapy
and Amulets

The ancients believed that jewels were powerful magnets, and that for those people with whom the gems were compatible, the stones were capable of transmitting health and well-being; or for those people for whom the stones were antagonistic, deterioration of health could result. In early times, in addition to gems, some metals were also credited with healing powers. Silversmiths, goldsmiths and those who worked with gems were ranked as equal in importance to apothecaries who dispensed herbs or drugs for health purposes. Today the art is being revived.

Many people consider the effect of gems pure superstition or possibly due to the power of suggestion. Others, however, believe that there is scientific justification for the effects of precious stones used for healing purposes which cannot be ignored. The late Howard Brenton MacDonald, M.D., of England, wrote:

Certain gems and precious stones and metals, to a lesser degree, act as condensers of cosmic energy from the sun and can thus focus this healing and powerful force on the bodies of people wearing them. Each kind of gem vibrates differently from the other, selecting and attracting different wave lengths or rates of vibrations to pass on to the wearer. For example, diamonds have one vibratory rate, rubies another, and emeralds still another, each apparently helping to correct a vibratory rate in the body and set up a new vibratory field around the body which may contribute to health.

Ann Ree Colton declares:

The belief that jewels contain amulet or protective powers is not a fallacy. Jeweled talisman power is a true science. Certain jewels correlate to certain planets as well as to zodiacal signs. The jewel correlating to one's birth or zodiacal sign is a powerful amulet protector.

The *Organic Consumer Report* has stated:[*]

Precious stones are today a status symbol, but centuries ago they were used as medicines for those who were wealthy enough to pay for the prescriptions. A limestone tablet in New York City's Metropolitan Museum dates back to 1500 B.C. Cleopatra is noted for having dissolved a priceless pearl in her wine to gain immortality . . . a property attributed to pearls in her times.

Necheps (640 B.C.) wore a jasper around his neck to cure his queasy stomach. Around 500 B.C. opals were used as a preventive for blindness. Emeralds were thought to protect children against epileptic fits, garnets to prevent bad blood. Many who survived the bubonic plague in Europe in the fourteenth century claimed they owed their lives to the wearing of such jewels as opals, rubies and sapphires. As late as the eighteenth century, apothecaries kept a

* Vol. 52, No. 39, Sept. 26, 1972. Compiled at Eden Ranch, P.O. Box 370, Topanga, California, 90290

quantity of pearls in stock, in powders, syrups and tinctures.

Pearls were considered so valuable as medicine that Pope Clement VII in 1531 ran up a high debt by drinking powdered pearls and other precious stones. He recovered. The idea of pearls having medicinal properties still persists today.

The readings of Edgar Cayce, the clairvoyant, insisted that gems do carry vibrations, but indicated that the same gems do not necessarily affect all people in the same way. If chosen correctly for the individual, however, they could benefit the wearer physically or mentally or increase spiritual attunement.

If you had not previously read about the effects of color in this book, the effects of gems might seem a figment of the imagination. Actually there is not a great deal of mystery to gem therapy for two reasons: first, each stone has a color which carries its own vibration or influence, as we have seen; and second, stones have been analyzed and are found to be *mineral* deposits. For example, there is the report that a strong light shining through an amethyst has created a fertilizing effect on plants, and light transmitted through an emerald has caused hair to grow in the ears of guinea pigs. In each case, if true, the *mineral involved* is no doubt responsible.

Further investigation reveals that amethyst is a clear quartz, ranging from purplish to blue-violet in color, has a chemical formula of SiO_2, and contains a trace of manganese, whereas the emerald's color is due to small amounts of chromium, and because it belongs to the beryl family, its chemical composition is that of beryl: $Be_3Al_2(SiO_3)_6$. So jewels are considered minerals!

It may also be true that jewels do take on the qualities of a magnet, and act as condensers with greater energy than the same minerals found in food, plants or other forms of color. At least Benoytosh Bhattacharyya, M.A., Ph.D., states, "The waves produced by metals and herbs are somewhat feeble and less efficient, though they have been employed successfully in minor cases. The gems have been found by experience to be the very best."

In India there is a centuries-old group of therapists, known as Ayurvedic physicians, who are required to have special training in order to practice their art. These physicians prepare some of their medicines from the ashes of gems which have been burned or powdered, and prescribe them in oral form for a variety of incurable diseases. One of my two daughters, both of whom have lived in India, talked with a well-educated granddaughter of the Minister of Health in one of the provinces, who told her that her grandfather had had his life prolonged by using gold and other minerals in Ayurvedic form.

Dr. Bhattacharyya explains, "Gems may be burned by a special process and their ashes may be used in medicine. Ashes of gems are sold in Ayurvedic pharmacies in India. Their rays are the ancient editions of modern isotopes."

Although the British at one time attempted to suppress the Ayurvedic art, the Indian Congress has recently voted funds for establishing an Ayurvedic Institute, which would be comparable in status to that of orthodox medicine.

Since burning or powdering precious stones is

admittedly expensive, is there any other way gems
can be employed for healing purposes? Dr. Bhattacharyya offers suggestions: "Gems can be used
as medicine in several ways. A gem kept in dis-
tilled water or alcohol for several days will cause
the liquid to be charged with the rays of the gem
and will prove to be a powerful medicine." David
V. Tansley, D.C., says:

Small, good quality gems are purchased and each is
placed in a glass vial containing a diluted alcohol
solution. This is placed in darkness for a week, allowing the vibratory force of the gem to permeate the
solution. At the end of a week, the gem is removed,
washed in water, dried and placed in storage for
future use. . . . These medicines can then be given
orally when indicated. The gems last forever so the
practitioner has the means to make his own medicines as the need arises, without going into any
complicated procedures. The mixtures may be mixed
to form combination remedies of several or all of
the gems.

Dr. Bhattacharyya adds, "Gems set in rings will
create a magnetic field around a person and will
eradicate evil including ill-health if worn rightly
and properly." The Cayce readings suggest, in
some cases, that better results for some people
would come from wearing the stone as a necklace
directly against the skin.

Are there any recent examples of the effects of
gem therapy? Although *any* information on gem
therapy is almost nonexistent, or at least very difficult to find, there has appeared a fascinating
article by Barbara Anton in *Fate* magazine (July
1969). Barbara Anton is a Graduate Gemologist
from the Gemological Institute of New York,

where she studied the scientific properties of the various gems. She also designs jewelry; many pieces have appeared in museums and art galleries in Europe, Asia and the United States. She is a writer and lecturer and has appeared on radio and TV.

Miss Anton tells of some of her personal experiences with the healing properties of gems. In agreement with the Cayce readings, which she also refers to, she admits that the same gems may not work in the same way for everyone. One of her clients had a daughter who had suffered from irregular menstrual periods since she was a teenager. No medical treatment had been effective. Miss Anton suggested a yellow jasper pendant on a chain to be worn directly on her skin. As long as the girl wore the necklace (which had been given to her by her mother without any explanation), the periods became exactly regular: 28 days apart. Later the periods suddenly became irregular again, and the mother learned that her daughter had broken the chain and had stopped wearing it. The mother told her daughter the reason for her gift, and the daughter had the chain repaired and put it on again. The periods immediately became regular once more.

In another case a nurse suffered from a leg pain. Miss Anton suggested that she wear a moonstone. As long as the nurse wore the stone, as a pendant, day and night, for over a year, the pain left. The nurse decided to stop wearing the stone and the pain reappeared. When she resumed wearing it, the pain again disappeared.

The moonstone figured in another of Miss Anton's reports. A seventy-eight-year-old woman, a primitive artist, was diagnosed by a doctor as having arthritis. She, too, obtained a moonstone, set in a pendant and worn on a 14-carat gold chain around her neck. She wore the pendant twenty-four hours a day for two years, during which time her pain disappeared. Later, she also broke the chain and did not wear the pendant for two months during which time the pain returned. She then had the chain repaired, wore the pendant once more, and the pain left.

How do you know which stone, if any, will help you? There is no sure-fire method except to study the properties of the various gems which follow, and use the trial-and-error method as your guide. If the use of a stone seems to help, you may want to continue; if it doesn't, experiment with another. Some people who are expert in using a pendulum can determine if a gem is right or wrong for them. (I have described the use of the pendulum in my book, *Get Well Naturally*.)* So look upon this forgotten art as a fascinating experiment and have fun. A trustworthy lapidary or gem cutter can probably provide you with an inexpensive collection of truly precious or semiprecious stones for experimental purposes. (Beware of glass or costume jewelry which are imitations of true gems.) The following fascinating gem lore information is drawn from the few books available on the subject, listed under the Bibliography.

A German mineralogist, Friedrich Mohs (1773-1839) devised a scale to determine the relative hardness of a mineral according to its resistance to scratching by one of the following minerals, arranged in order from the softest to the hardest:

* Linda Clark: *Get Well Naturally*. The Devin-Adair Co., Old Greenwich, Conn. 06870, second printing, 1974

1. Talc	6. Feldspar
2. Gypsum	7. Quartz
3. Calcite	8. Topaz
4. Fluorite	9. Sapphire
5. Apatite	10. Diamond

Thus nothing can scratch a diamond, while any
other mineral will scratch talc. A Mohs scale or
hardness reading of 7.5, for example, means that
the mineral will scratch quartz but cannot mar
topaz.

AGATE

Agate has a hardness rating of 7. It is formed
from silica deposits and its chemical formula is
SiO_2. It is said to help harden gums. Since silica
is now known to aid the assimilation of calcium,
this may be one explanation. The ancients believed that agates protected the vision.

AMBER

The Mohs scale rating for amber is from 2 to
2.5. It is not a mineral, but rather a form of fossil-
ized resin from antediluvian pine trees, and is
classified under names such as puccinite, ruminite,
burmite or pimetite. Its electrical healing properties were revered by the ancients. If worn around
the neck it was supposed to calm nerves. Ground
up with honey and rose oil and taken internally,
it was considered a specific for deafness. Ground
up with honey alone it was supposed to improve
dimness of eyes. Amber is also claimed to be help-

ful for dysentery and throat afflictions. Dr. Howard Brenton MacDonald wrote, "My wife is a concert singer and wore a necklace of genuine amber, feeling that it helped quiet her nerves and soothe her throat during a concert." According to Barbara Anton, amber is also credited with aiding liver, kidneys, and diseases of throat, head, catarrh, goiter, asthma and hay fever. Since amber's original source is pine trees, rich in vitamin C which is considered helpful in many of the above diseases, the explanation may not be entirely farfetched.

AMETHYST

Amethyst, with the hardness rating of quartz (7) and the same chemical formula (SiO_2) as agate, is a clear quartz ranging from purple to blue-violet in color. Some people have believed that wearing amethyst is warming to the body, expels poisons, and is an antidote to drunkenness. Amethysts were also believed to guarantee peace of mind.

BERYL

Beryl is usually green, though it may be yellow, green, blue or white. Its hardness rating is 7.5 to 8 and its chemical composition ($Be_3Al_2(SiO_3)_6$), is the same as emerald. It is supposed to alleviate complaints of the diaphragm and liver.

BLOODSTONE

Bloodstone, or heliotrope, is massive quartz with small drops of jasper which resemble drops of blood. It may occur in different shades of green, with a hardness rating of 7 and a composition of SiO_2. The "drop-of-blood" appearance has long convinced gem lovers of its successful use for hemorrhages. It is claimed that if suspended from the neck it will prevent nosebleeds.

CARNELIAN

Because of its resemblance to blood, carnelian is also believed to ward off hemorrhages, stop nosebleeds and purify blood. It is another form of quartz or chalcedony.

CHRYSOLITE

Chrysolite is usually olive green but may occur in browns, yellows and reds. Its hardness rating is 6 to 7. It is a silicate of magnesium and iron, and its chemical formula is $(MgFe)_2SiO_4$. If set in gold, chrysolite was said by the Egyptians to prevent fever and nightmares and provide protection from evil spirits. It is also called peridot.

CORAL

Coral is, of course, made of skeletons of tiny sea animals, with a hardness rating of 3.5. Its chemical composition is mainly calcium carbonate ($CaCO_3$). Though not a gem in the strict sense of the word, it is considered a semi-precious stone in some instances.

Red coral is supposed to stop general bleeding. White coral, along with red coral, is said to stop the flow of blood from wounds.

Plato stated that the best coral, if worn on the neck, will reflect the heat of the person who wears it. He also said, if the person is sick, the coral will become pale and wan, but will return to its normal color when the person's health is restored.

Coral is also claimed to be a help in digestive disorders and epilepsy in children. The Romans used it in salves for ulcers, scars and sore eyes. According to Dr. Bhattacharyya, Ayurveda ashes of coral taken internally can increase beauty, help emaciation and rickets, cough, loss of appetite, indigestion, constipation, fevers, poisons, insanity, anemia, jaundice, urinary diseases, eye troubles, asthma and obesity.

There are some warnings not to wear brown or dirty, discolored corals. These are supposed to encourage evil spirits.

DIAMOND

The diamond is the hardest substance known, with a rating of 10. It is pure carbon (C). When viewed through a prism, it appears indigo blue. In the human body indigo influences coughs and mucus as well as the lymph system. However, according to Dr. Bhattacharyya, the diamond is a good medicine for all sorts of diseases. He says that the diamond taken internally "prolongs life, strengthens the body, nourishes the tissues, improves the complexion" and is of help to many other disturbances. Barbara Anton agrees that diamonds are one of the worst enemies of disease, "curing everything from toothache to convulsions and insomnia," either by being worn, or rubbed on the afflicted area, or by drinking water magnetized by them.

Edgar Cayce has mentioned in one reading that the diamond is a "selfish" stone, and can bring either peace or irritation to the wearer. The Hindus believed that an *imperfect* diamond could cause trouble. So you will have to learn for yourself the effect of the diamond for *you*. If it seems to prove beneficial, use it; but as Edgar Cayce warns, do not become a slave to *any* stone. There are others forms of healing in nature and we should take advantage of them all.

EMERALD

Emerald is a clear, green variety of beryl with the same characteristics—hardness: 7.5 to 8, and the chemical formula $Be_3Al_2(SiO_3)_6$. A trace of chromic oxide gives it its color. However, the emerald is a more valuable stone than other beryls and has some exciting therapeutic properties to its credit, according to historical lore. Emeralds were found to be an antidote for poisons and the Egyptians used them for treatment of eye diseases. Egyptian women were noted for their superior eyesight. According to Barbara Anton, the Romans also believed the emerald would protect one from evil spirits as well as rest and refresh the eyes. They believed that a helpful eyewash could be made by steeping the emerald in water.

Since green is the color of abundance in nature, the ancient belief is that the emerald is a symbol of abundance and immortality and helps to promote all well-being. Hippocrates used the emerald in his healing work.

GARNET

The garnet has a hardness rating of 6.5 to 7.5. It is a legendary heart stimulant. Gazing at a garnet was believed in early times also to lead to passion, anger, even apoplexy. The deep red form is the most valuable as a gem.

JADE

Jade is a hard, tough silicate with a hardness rating of 6.5 to 7; Orientals consider it a sacred stone. It is said to be a prophylactic for kidney disease, stomach pains and lungs, as well as having the ability to purify the blood and strengthen the muscles.

According to Barbara Anton's research, it protects its wearer against diseases of many kinds, accidents and witchcraft; is helpful for urinary problems, and promotes a long life with a peaceful end. She states that jade worn next to the skin was supposed to ward off disease as well as the "evil eye." One of its greatest boons is apparently the effect on eyes. Like the emerald, the green color was believed to strengthen and improve the eyes. The belief was that it could be accomplished by holding the jade directly on the eyelids, or steeping it in water and using the water as an eyewash.

Ann Ree Colton states that concentrating on jade in meditation can draw pranic energy into one's consciousness.

JASPER

Jasper was used in ancient times to cure a queasy stomach and soothe nervousness. It is a green form of quartz, uncrystalline, that occurs in other shades as well.

LAPIS

Lapis lazuli, or lazurite, or lapis linguis ranges in color from rich deep blue to azure, violet-blue or green-blue. Its hardness is 5 to 5.5 and the chemical formula is $3NAl\ SiO_4.Na_2S$. It is a mixture of various minerals and is usually found in limestone near granite. The ancient physicians used them for eye troubles. Early alchemists considered lapis a stone that helps attune one to the higher spiritual vibrations. The Cayce readings pointed out that lapis lazuli, because of its strong vibrations of elements which encourage strength and vitality, should be encased in plastic or crystal or layers of glass before being worn around the neck or the wrist; otherwise the radiation is too great.

Lapis ligurius, also known as malachite, is a carbonate of copper with a hardness of 3.5 to 4, and a chemical composition of $CuCO_3Cu\ (OH)_2$. As early as 4000 B.C. the Egyptians were mining it and using it for the treatment of cholera, rheumatism and protection from the "evil eye."

MOONSTONE

The moonstone resembles an opal; its hardness is 6; it is a form of feldspar, and its chemical composition is $KAlSi_3O_8$. In Ceylon, where it is found in abundance, it is called the "Ceylon Opal." One fine specimen of a moonstone, owned by Pope Leo X (1475–1521) appeared to be dull when the moon was old, increasing in brilliance as the moon increased from new to full. The moonstone was considered by ancient physicians as a protection against dropsy and "watery disturbances." To some, it is supposed to give strength. Moonstone is actually considered a light blue.

OPAL

Opal is composed of silica and water: SiO_2. NH_2O, and ranges between 5.5 to 6.5 in hardness. There are several types of opals—precious opal, which has more delicate colorings, fire opal with fire-like red-to-yellow streaks of color, and black opal with a dark green background. It is said to help the heart and strengthen weak eyes.

The opal is a somewhat controversial stone since it is thought to bring bad luck except if it is one's birthstone (Libra). Someone asked Edgar Cayce to clarify this. The readings stated that those who have fire signs in their aura should never wear opals nor even flowers on their bodies since they will fade. A different reading said that the opal for those who are *not* born in Libra (and for whom it is not their birthstone) can be helpful in controlling temper. For others, the readings stated that a fire opal can provide vigor, understanding and purification, but that it carries great intenseness.

One ancient belief was that an opal turned pale in the presence of poisons, lost its lustre in the presence of the wearer's enemies, but radiated with joy at the appearance of friends. Even so, the admonishment from these early sages was "use the opal sparingly."

However, the opal, according to Ann Ree Colton, is a protective stone with planetary energy. It provides protection, justice, harmony and depth to the emotions. After the bubonic plague in Europe in the fourteenth century, many who survived claimed that they owed their lives to the wearing of opals, rubies and sapphires.

PEARL

The pearl has a chemical formula of $CaCO_3$ plus organic matter. Pearls emit an orange ray and have attracted a great deal of attention throughout the ages. Since they are formed within the shell of a mollusk, usually an oyster, they represent protection from irritation. According to the Cayce readings, those who wear pearls, like those who wear diamonds, will be either soothed or irritated. The chemical composition of pearl is about ninety-two carbonate of calcium, six percent organic substance, and the rest (two percent) water. The hardness ranges from 2.5 to 4.5. Since this is a calcium-like composition, it makes sense that very early physicians ground pearls into a powder, added it to milk and prescribed it for irritability. Today we know that calcium allays irritability, but according to the Cayce readings, though the pearl has developed under stress, its emanations are a symbol for protection against the hardships that produced the beauty of the pearl.

Ann Ree Colton states, "The pearl is a jewel made through irritation between water and sand playing upon the life mass in an oyster. In human life the pearl represents victory over self-made tribulation."

In the 18th century, pearls began to be used in powdered form as medicine to replace leeches. They were sold for high prices for this purpose.

The pearl has always been considered one of the most beautiful of all gems, representing faith and purity and is said to soften violence and anger.

Lustreless pearls are considered unfortunate.

RUBY

Ruby is next to the diamond in hardness. It is a corundum, or aluminum oxide, with the formula, Al_2O_3.

The Hindus consider it the most valuable gem of all, and it is supposed to be more fortunate if worn on the left hand or the l∙ 't side of the body. The ruby, according to Dr. Bhattacharyya, releases red cosmic waves and is capable of healing diseases connected with cold. The Ayurvedic ashes of ruby are used for tuberculosis, pain, colic, boils, ulcers, effects of poisons, eye troubles and constipation. Others consider it good for flatulence, biliousness and general body health.

Barbara Anton states that in India rubies are taped to the forehead because they are believed to influence thinking, or if placed under the pillow, they are said to induce peaceful, pleasant dreams.

The ancients believed that rubies guard against infectious diseases. Ann Ree Colton considers the ruby a healing jewel for the blood.

SARDONYX

Sardonyx, a form of onyx, has a hardness rating of 7, with a chemical composition SiO_2. Its colors vary from clear red, brownish red, or black. Its colors are probably influenced by various amounts of iron. The properties of this stone seem to have mental and emotional rather than physical effects. According to the sages it encourages happiness and good fortune and banishes grief, and it releases an ultraviolet ray. Onyx is said to help eyes and arrest hemorrhages.

SAPPHIRE

Sapphire is violet in color, and is another variety of corundum. It is considered good for eyes and boils. The Ayurvedic physicians use ashes of sapphires for rheumatism, colic and mental diseases. Sapphires were supposed to guard against evil thoughts.

TOPAZ

Topaz is a mineral with a hardness rating of 8. Its formula is $Al_2(FOH)_2SiO_4$. It occurs in granite deposits and its color can vary from yellows through white, green, blue or red, with a vitreous lustre. It is said to release strong electric emanations and to help dimness of vision, hemorrhages and bleeding of wounds.

TURQUOISE

Little is known about turquoise except that its hardness is 6 and its composition is phosphate of copper and aluminum. It is blue, green, or blue-green, either translucent or opaque. It is said to strengthen the eyes, to be a symbol of youth, and to prevent a violent death.

There are other stones, of course, but little or nothing is known of their healing powers. Lobsang Rampa, the Tibetan Lama, states that gems have very strong vibrations and act like radio transmitters, transmitting good or bad messages at all times. Dr. Bhattacharyya adds that the major gems—ruby, pearl, coral, emerald, moonstone, diamond and sapphire are inexhaustible sources of cosmic rays.

CALENDAR OF BIRTH STONES

Month	Ancient	Modern
January	Garnet	Garnet

Month	Ancient	Modern
February	Amethyst	Amethyst
March	Jasper	Bloodstone or Aquamarine
April	Sapphire	Diamond
May	Agate	Emerald
June	Emerald	Pearl, Moonstone or Alexandrite
July	Onyx	Ruby
August	Carnelian	Sardonyx or Carnelian
September	Chrysolite	Sapphire
October	Aquamarine	Opal or Tourmaline
November	Topaz	Topaz
December	Ruby	Turquoise or Zircon

Source: Retail Jewelers of America, Inc. If your
local jeweler cannot supply gemstones, write S. N.
Green, Bayfield, Colorado 81122 for his catalog.

AMULETS

At the present time there is a woman in the
United States who is doing some exciting work
with gems which she fashions into attractive amulets to be used for various problems. You may
choose a love-and-fulfillment amulet, a money-
and-profits amulet, a health-and-tranquility amulet, or an all-powerful amulet (also known as the
problem-solver amulet), which combines all three:
love, money and health. The health amulet is internationally famous and perhaps the most popular of them all. Jeannie Lemmay, an artist and the
originator of this unique idea, has made over ten
thousand amulets over the past seventeen years

and states that they cannot be copied; the secret remains hers and hers alone.

She says, "My amulets are friendly, harmonious to all religions; I think of them as calming, beautiful sources of universal power. What I do to get them to work is my own private function that I perform in my inner sanctum. That is why my amulets are famous; they work."

Mrs. Lemmay, an attractive blonde mother of two teen-agers, describes the properties of her amulets, but makes no claims about what they can do, or have done. She leaves that to the enthusiastic users who agree that they do work. People write her to tell her how beautiful their amulets are, and of their successes in using them, whether it be acquiring a new husband (one amulet brought success to four generations in one family), success with court proceedings, increase in income or improvement of health. Jeannie told me that doctors and physiotherapists have confirmed physical improvement in their patients after receiving an amulet. As a matter of fact, many M.D.s and psychiatrists order amulets for themselves, says Jeannie, the former wife of an M.D. who also used one of her amulets.

Jeannie Lemmay not only believes in the benefits of her amulets, she is truly concerned about helping people with them, in some cases custom-making them to fit individual needs. Although she vehemently denies that the amulets are astrological, occult or imbued with witchcraft (she refuses to make one which will hurt someone else), she does admit to being the granddaughter of a famous clairvoyant and to be being intuitive herself, which apparently helps her in matching up the right stones for different people and their needs. When

I asked her about her percentage of failures, she answered promptly, "One failure in a thousand, and that one distresses me very much." She has offered to take back any amulet which has not worked, and to date has few takers.

In addition to being beautiful, the amulets are rare examples of a unique art. Mrs. Lemmay makes them from stones acquired from all over the world. For instance, she chooses agates that are millions of years old. For the amulet base she chooses natural materials from fifty-two exotic types of wood. This she tops with a flat white disk, hand decorated with her own brand of hieroglyphics in 22-carat gold. This is then crowned with a gem to help the person, the problem or both. She seems to connect intuitively with the person for whom she is making the amulet and takes her assignment very seriously. It requires a week to one month to complete it following an order.*

The amulet can be pinned to a garment, placed in a pocket or worn on a chain. Jeannie Lemmay believes that, though it is not necessary to wear it, it should be kept near you, perhaps in a desk drawer, or at night on your bedside table or under your pillow. In order to activate the amulet, she instructs you—on receiving it—to give a friend or relative $1.00 plus one penny, which represents 101 good wishes to others, a symbol of giving before receiving. She states that after that, the amulet is ready to go, although it may take from an hour up to three weeks to begin working.

Is the effect of the amulet psychological? Per-

---

* For brochure, description and prices of amulets, write Jeannie Lemmay, P.O. Box 1011, San Juan Capistrano, California 92675

haps. But after reading in the early part of this chapter of the ancients' belief in the effect of vibrations of various stones, the effect may also be physical. I have found that wearing an amulet seems to bring your desires to you in unexpected ways. As Jeannie says, it can't hurt you, and it is worth a try. In any event you will acquire a conversation piece in the form of a beautiful piece of jewelry. And if you are one of those who achieve other benefits as well, you may discover that the ancients were right: gems do indeed have their own power.

11. Auras

Originally, I did not plan to mention ESP in connection with color in this book. But after the manuscript was finished and the word spread that a book on color therapy was about to be published, I was besieged with requests for information on auras. More and more people, it seems, are beginning to see auras and do not know how to interpret them. A friend would say, "I see such and such a color around Mary, or Lucy, or John. What does this color mean when it appears in the aura?"

Audrey Kargere, Ph.D., states in her book, *Color and Personality*, "There was a well-known judge who could often tell the general character of a speaker's thoughts, before they were even spoken, from the colors of the emanations he saw around his head. There are many people who can see colors around persons and objects but do not know their meaning."

Since many people have shown even more interest in this subject than in the colors used for clothes or interior decorating or healing, I was literally sent scurrying to research sources in order to find some answers.

Those who are fortunate enough to see auras state that every living thing has an aura: people, a tree, a flower, an animal, even a rock. In people, the aura apparently hugs the body, radiating outward at various distances, according to the individual. This aura is made up of various colors which seem to impart information concerning the spiritual development of the individual, as well to reflect their health and emotions.

The major color which represents the spiritual development seems to be more or less stable, whereas the colors representing a person's health and emotions appear to fluctuate according to the current conditions experienced by the person. For example, if someone is fearful or depressed, the colors may be muddy. If the health is vibrant, the colors seem to be clear. If vitality is low, the colors may appear diluted; if vitality is high, the colors may be brilliant. According to those who have long worked with auras, if you see a break in the aura, apparently there is an energy leak from the body at that point.

As I have reported elsewhere,* there is speculation that the day will come when doctors, either through their own ability to see auras, or with the help of an instrument (so far not available) will be able to diagnose physical conditions before they appear. The condition can then hopefully be reversed by the use of a missing or corrective color. This is not mere conjecture. The Kirlians, man and wife, in Russia, have already photographed auras in color† and a recent report states

---

* Linda Clark: *Help Yourself to Health.* Pyramid Publications, New York, 1972

† Sheila Ostrander and Lynn Schroeder; *Psychic Discoveries Behind The Iron Curtain.* Bantam, paperback edition, 1971

that a similar technique of recording auras is under way at some American universities.

I have known clairvoyants who see auras automatically. I knew Edgar Cayce personally, and he told me that he had always seen auras around people and supposed everyone else saw them too. It was his opinion that a person's favorite color was his major aura color, which explains why one is attracted to that particular color or its components. I did not tell him my favorite color until I asked him what my aura color was. He was right; the two matched exactly!

Only recently have I learned that many average people are beginning to see auras for the first time and are slightly bewildered by the phenomenon. I chose several at random and queried them to see if a pattern existed which would throw light on the subject for others. The one common denominator of these people appeared to be that they are all interested in spiritual growth and development, though their religions vary. They believe in prayer and are striving to become better people, helpful to others and trying to live by the golden rule.

An older woman told me she had seen only light and dark around people, not colors. At first she thought something was wrong with her eyes and she would try to blink away the light. Also, at first, the light appeared as faint, but gradually became more intense. She saw this light around people with her eyes open (not everyone does). She told me that the soloist in the church which she attends seemed to be surrounded with the brightest light she had yet seen. She also saw a dark aura surrounding an elderly person who later passed on.

A young married woman sees colors around many people, but not all. Mostly she notices these auras around those who are highly developed spiritually, such as certain ministers, religious teachers, and clairvoyants. She, like others, states that if she looks for auras, she does not see them; they just appear, and she does not see them at all unless she is "centered." She explained this as meaning that she stills her mind and emotions as in meditation and tries to think of herself as a channel, not an egotistical individual. The auras this woman sees are translucent and iridescent.

A successful businessman with a family told me he has seen auras for five years and that at first he thought everyone saw them and he was merely a late-comer. This man began by seeing auras only with his eyes closed as he concentrated on the person before him. Now he is beginning to see the auras with his eyes open, or even if he is only thinking of the person. He sees the colors as more solid than transparent, but arranged in layers somewhat like a rainbow. He finds that some colors in people's auras may change over a period of years. At the moment he is concerned because he has seen an aura with lightning-like flashes of black around a young man. He assumes that this means a poor health problem or a forthcoming danger which he is unable to interpret. He, too, says he must be "centered" within himself in order to see auras and always prays before looking for an aura. He added that he refuses to look at the auras of the members of his immediate family because he feels he is too close to them to be objective.

A psychological therapist, whom I met only recently, came to my house with a friend. We were all in the kitchen preparing some snacks when suddenly she said she saw a certain color around me and asked me what it meant. It turned out to be the same color Mr. Cayce saw around me! On questioning her further, she, too, told me she cannot see auras if she *tries* to see them. They come unexpectedly when she isn't even thinking about them and usually are noticeable around people who are especially high-powered spiritually.

Another woman, interested in healing, sees auras only in those who seem to have strong healing ability. Usually, she says, she sees the colors out of the corner of her eye as they stream from the person's hands or arms. If she looks directly at these elusive colors, they promptly disappear and she must wait until they appear of their own accord. She cannot force them to appear.

I have listed the meaning of the colors usually found in the aura at the end of the chapter as supplied by those experienced in reading auras. They may give you a clue to the condition of the person whom you are witnessing. Also, one can deliberately visualize certain colors around someone in need. The Rosicrucians, whose metaphysical knowledge has existed for many centuries, contribute such a formula. They state that if a person you know is suffering from emotional problems which are causing an ailment, you can visualize a pink or a rosy-pink surrounding him. This pink color should be accompanied by a feeling of love. However, if the condition seems to be due to a rundown physical cause, you can visualize a bright orange color surrounding him.*

* Joseph J. Weed: *Wisdom of the Mystic Masters.* Parker Publishing Co., West Nyack, New York, eighth printing, 1970

In addition to other self-helps suggested throughout this book, several people hav told me of the good results they have achieved by visualizing the rainbow on themselves and others. White, of course, includes all colors; black usually represents the absence of color. However, the theory is that the rainbow contains all of the color components and, if visualized around your own body or that of another, it may help it to draw the correct color from the rainbow which is needed at the moment.

One businesswoman says that she wraps herself mentally (by visualization) with a spiral rainbow from head to foot before she leaves her house in the morning. She says that everywhere she goes people whom she has never met stop her and say "Hi! How are you today?" as if she were an old friend. Her explanation is that the rainbow must radiate and attract others. When she does not use the rainbow, people do not notice her.

In another instance, a young housewife says she has learned by trial and error to put the rainbow on—also in spiral form—from head to foot before she gets out of bed in the morning. Before she began to do this, she would be greeted on her arrival in the kitchen by an irritable and grumbling family: husband *and* children. After adopting the rainbow habit, she says it is incredible but true that the grumbling has changed to cheerfulness. Still another young woman says she does the same thing before leaving her house on a shopping tour. Otherwise she feels a drain of energy as she mingles with people. Protected by the rainbow of colors, she insists she does not become depleted.

If you are one of the lucky ones who already

see auras, but do not know how to interpret them, the following list of the meaning of aura colors may help you. If you need further help, you may wish to read some of the booklets from which these colors were taken. They are listed in the Bibliography and were written by those who have had extensive experience in reading auras.

WHITE

A white aura is considered the highest of all. All colors are blended into white. White is another name for light and represents a purifying, uplifting and sterilizing vibration. It also is considered a symbol of the wisdom of Divine Power and thus the most healing of all color vibrations. The more dazzling the white, the higher the vibration.

There are many shades of white, although I will list only three:

Pearl white represents kindness, gentleness and forgiveness.

Oyster white indicates that the soul is trying hard to unfold in spite of tests and lessons being experienced.

Crystal white indicates that the soul has acquired complete self-mastery. This is extremely rare.

RED

Although the shade determines its true meaning, in general, red stands for energy, strength, courage, vitality. It is the badge of determination and perseverance. It is also the color of sacrifice; the giving of oneself, and is thus combined with green as Christmas colors.

S.G.J. Ouseley states, "People with a great deal of red in their auras have strong physical propensities, strong minds and wills, and usually a materialistic outlook on life. They often manifest a very warm and affectionate nature. Red can also denote, however, the deepest of human passions whether passionate love, courage, hatred or revenge."

Dark red means physical vitality only; not mental or spiritual strength.

Rose red indicates love of family and country.

Bright, clear red symbolizes faith, hope and courage.

Dark, muddy or cloudy red is mixed with negative conditions, such as nervousness, temper, even domineering qualities and possibly strife.

Scarlet may indicate egotism.

Medium orange-red is a healing, vitalizing color and is often seen emanting from the hands and fingers of many healers, including especially conscientious medical doctors.

PINK

Pink, especially salmon pink, is the color of universal love. Depending on the shade of pink, it can supply or encourage joy and comfort, as well as companionship. People are drawn warmly to those who wear pink.

Pink is also the color of human love. Used for others it can be uplifting, joyful and a key to abundance. In the aura, coral can mean a feeling of unsureness about decisions and/or unhappiness in one's surroundings.

S.G.J. Ouseley writes, "A pink aura denotes a quiet, refined, modest type of character who likes a quiet life, beauty and artistic surroundings. People of the pink-aura type will exhibit great and lasting devotion, are rarely positive, dogmatic or aggressive."

ORANGE

Orange varies with the shade. Usually orange represents thoughtfulness and consideration. Yogis call orange the "soul of energy." Those with orange in their auras are leaders who tactfully manage others and are excellent mixers. They are the "live-wire" type, yet well-balanced.

Golden orange represents wisdom and energy and can increase mental and spiritual ability. It is considered a high, spiritual vibration, and denotes self-control.

Brownish orange may mean a lack of ambition, laziness or repression.

According to Edgar Cayce, those with orange in their auras should watch out for kidney trouble.

YELLOW

Yellow represents health of body and mind; the more golden yellow, the better. Yellow is the easiest auric color to see; it is close to the hairline.

Ouseley believes that yellow, except for muddy shades, is a good aspect in the aura. The golden shades symbolize not only thought, intellect and mental concentration, but also things of the spirit represented in religious ceremonies, such as golden crosses, vessels and altar fittings.

According to Ouseley, yellow is beneficial in dispelling fear, worry, nervousness and is stimulating to health and mind. Yellow appears in the auras of bright and optimistic people, he adds.

Yellow mixed with red indicates timidity. If redheads have yellow in their aura, they may have an inferiority complex, be indecisive, or followers instead of leaders.

Lemon yellow indicates mental strength, or artistic, creative ability leaning toward scientific ideas and inventions.

Very pale lemon yellow may indicate sickness in the body.

BLUE

There are many shades of blue, all of them good, but different shades have different qualities. Blue is the color of healing love, which is soothing.

Ouseley says, "Blue represents inspiration; it is the spiritual color. The presence of much blue in the aura signifies artistic, harmonious nature with spiritual understanding. The darker shades of blue, especially, show a high degree of spirituality, integrity, deep sincerity, wisdom and saintliness."

Pale blue represents less maturity but a strong desire to acquire it.

Madonna blue is the color of obedience and fulfillment of duties, as in the obedience to the will of God.

Deep, rich royal blue is more powerful than the

lighter shades. It indicates honesty, loyalty, and if it contains a tinge of purple, good judgment and an ability to handle material affairs efficiently. Those who have deep blue in their auras are highly involved in their chosen work, or are unselfishly dedicated to social causes, science or art. Such people are also spiritually inclined.

When black or brown is mixed with blue, it causes heavy-heartedness. The vibrations are lowered and can lead to the remark, "I feel blue."

GREEN

Just as green shoots indicate new growth and hope, green symbolizes newness, continuity of life, peace, abundance and healing. Doctors and nurses often have green in their auras, and it is a strong, friendly, helpful color, indicating loving service, cooperation, goodness, mercy, hope, faith and peace. It is calming, restful to the nerves and good for overcoming fear.

S.G.J. Ouseley says, "If nervous, highly strung people realized the beneficial effects of green on the mind and nerves, they would surround themselves with this soothing color. Its vibrations are extremely refreshing."

Edgar Cayce warns against greeny-yellow, which he calls "gaslight green." He says he has never seen it to fail as a clue to untruth, evasion, and other forms of deceit. As green tends more toward blue, it becomes more trustworthy and helpful.

AQUA

Pure emerald green with a tinge of blue is a healing color. True aqua, which blends blue and green in equal parts, is high in vibrations. It combines peace and healing love, fills one with high ideals and is quieting for the nervous system.

VIOLET, PURPLE AND INDIGO

Lavender (pale purple) is a color of humility and worship.

Orchid (slightly more pink) is holy and spiritual.

Purple indicates an ability to deal with practical and worldly matters.

Indigo and violet in the aura show that a person is searching for a cause or religious experience, though those with purple in their aura are often overbearing.

Blue-purple represents accomplishments through God's power.

Red-purple indicates power of body, human will, and individual effort, a lower vibration than the blue-purple.

Edgar Cayce has stated that those who have indigo, violet and purple in their auras tend to heart and stomach troubles. Purple and indigo can also mean spiritual seeking or indicate that spiritual power is on the increase.

S.G.J. Ouseley believes that the violet ray is seldom seen in the average aura, since it is a highly spiritual color. He believes that its presence means true greatness and unselfish efforts.

GRAY

Those with a gray aura are persistent plodders who leave no task undone. They may also be the "lone wolf" type who like to live their lives in their own way.

Edgar Cayce stated that gray is the color of illness. When it is mixed with black it becomes heavier, vibrationally, dull and heavy. Gray has also long been known to indicate grief, sorrow and loss. However, it can be transmuted by adding red, or pink or blue to raise its vibration and become more peaceful, more harmonious. Silver is better than gray, since it contains a sparkle, which gray lacks.

BROWN

Brown is symbolic of the earth and there are many shades which are beautified by the addition of other colors, such as red, yellow or gold. If rich in color, brown is symbolic of growth, effort, and the wish to accomplish.

Brown stands for industry, organization and orderly management. According to S.G.J. Ouseley, it is the businessman's color, the ruling color of convention. Do not expect strong emotional feelings or tendencies in brown-tinged auras, but rather painstaking perseverance.

BLACK

It is true that there are various shades of black, depending on what colors have been added to it (blue, purple, silver, gold, etc.). However, black has the lowest vibration of all colors and should be shunned because of its heavy, dark influence. According to Ouseley, "Beware of black which seems to glow with crimson red shot with black. It is the most vicious combination of evil known."

If you are required to wear black in connection with your work, then brighten it up with a scarf or tie of some bright color. There are predictions that black will eventually be completely replaced with brighter, lighter colors of all hues and shades.

As Edgar Cayce has stated, we show more white (the opposite of black) in our auras as we grow toward perfection. This should be our goal.

Edgar Cayce wrote an essay on auras, his last written work. In it he stated, "An aura is an effect, not a cause . . . Thus at any time, in any world, a soul will give off, through the vibrations, the story of itself and the conditions in which it now exists."

Those who can see auras can read this message. Those who cannot, will not see the message, but the vibrations and colors are there, nevertheless. The Kirlian type photography has proved this to be true.

12. Breathing Color

The following article by Keith Ayling* opens a whole new field in color therapy:

Is it really possible to stop the clock of physical aging and look, feel and act as we did in our twenties and thirties?

Yvonne Martine of Gary, Indiana, says it is and proves it conclusively with her shapely body and pretty, unlined face, which she asserts was a mass of age wrinkles a few years back.

A grandmother and the proud mother of a handsome four-year-old boy, Yvonne is touching fifty. She has accomplished her seeming miracle of reversing the aging process with what she describes as help from above. Because of this she has dedicated her busy life to passing on to others her methods of remaking the body by her system of breathing in color.

The secret was revealed to her in a vision. Not a dream, but a waking vision, which directed her to study. By following the cosmic directions she has not only restored herself to a vivid, scintillating youthfulness but has done the same for others, men as well

* Reprinted from *Occult* magazine, October, 1972, © 1972 by Popular Library Publishers, a unit of Columbia Broadcasting System, Inc.

as women, by teaching what she calls a natural science of living.

"I've learned not to be discouraged when people think I am the product of a beauty parlor—or that I am slightly off the beam," she says. "I know I have something that can benefit humanity and I'm willing to help any who want to learn."

Once widowed and twice divorced, Yvonne with her svelte, shapely 98-pound figure could easily pass for twenty-five. Her pert, bright-eyed face (on which she uses a minimum of makeup) is devoid of wrinkles. Her hands, always tell-tale of a woman's age, are as smooth as a young girls, although she does her own housework in addition to directing a modeling and charm school, organizing floor shows for night spots, modeling furs and doing fashion talks on radio and TV.

With such a crowded schedule, you might expect the lady to have developed executive worry lines on her face. However, a microscope couldn't turn them up, for they simply aren't there. Yvonne is a vivid demonstration of her own teaching. She is one of those women at whom both sexes give a second glance in the street or in a restaurant. She emanates a definite magnetism which defies definition.

"How do you do it?" I asked her.

"I simply breathe pink as I told you," she replied with an amused almost compassionate smile. "Every morning and every night. It restores you. I don't have an acceptable physical explanation—only myself and the people I have been able to help. Doctors notice the change in people, but they don't know how it happens. You should see their faces when I tell them I breathe pink."

I met Yvonne through one of her pupils, a woman I had known twenty-five years ago. I mistook this woman for her daughter. In fact, she looked younger than when I had first met her. As she was telling me how she had taken Yvonne's advice, I found myself calculating she must be at least fifty, even if she looked half that age.

"You should see Yvonne," she said, "and some of her pupils." I took a plane to Gary, Indiana. The first sight of Yvonne proved she was not a figment of the imagination. She is real.

Yvonne's story is simple. "I was getting and looking old and not liking myself. I noticed many other women getting older and not liking it either. I saw them going around with quiet desperation in their eyes and using all those obvious little makeup tricks.

"I decided there must be a way to beat the years— or at least to lick premature aging. At that time I had just lost my husband and looked dreadful. Also I had become a kind of recluse, reading, meditating, searching and praying.

"Then it happened. One night I had what you might call a vision. I sat up in bed to find the room glowing with pink light radiating from a bright pink ball which had floated in through the window. As I looked at it tongue-tied and wide-eyed with wonder, but completely unafraid, the message came into my mind. I was to breathe pink.

"Naturally, it left me puzzled. I had studied yoga breathing and knew of its bright white light. But why the color? I read everything I could lay my hands on, as much as I could about the life force which enters us as we breathe in a certain way, and its enormous benefits.

"Three weeks later the ball of pink light came again, larger and brighter this time. The message was more emphatic. I was to keep on breathing pink.

"I realized then that I had something precious and wonderful, and began to study seriously and learn all I could about colors and its effect on our minds and bodies. This opened up an entire new field of research. I discovered I was able to apply the benefits of other colors in helping myself and others.

"I learned that psychiatrists know the value of color in treating various forms of mental illness, that some colors stimulate and others subdue. I learned that colors have vibration and possess qualities to heal pain and change a human personality, and that some, when combined with esoteric breathing, can be used to attract a certain type of person to you, whether it is for romantic, social or business reasons. I also found that inbreathing of a certain color combined with the correct audible vibrations—each color has its own—could revive sexual vigor."

After making this vitally important discovery, Yvonne decided to devote her life to bettering herself and to helping others to live happier and healthier lives.

"It wasn't anything I could rush," she says. "It took time. It took me eight or nine months to change myself. My mirror began to tell me I was looking better and my body began to change. So did my spirits. I stopped having those "blue Mondays" that so often affect us. Of course when people didn't recognize me at first sight I knew I was really making progress. The question was: how far could I go in this mystical rejuvenation treatment. You see, I was pioneering—exploring, you might say. Sometimes I wondered if I was kidding myself but the results were always there to prove I was making progress.

"One day, after a friend had laughingly told me I looked about twenty-five and that I had better stop or I would have to go back to high school, I took stock of myself, a long hard look as it were. Something had really happened. My sagging chin, the bags under my eyes and the deep lines on each side of my mouth had gone. Even those brown aging spots on my hands had disappeared. I really had something! Now I was ready to help other people.

"All this had brought a new life to me—or shall I describe it as a new and glorious interest in life itself. Gone were my aches and pains. The outward and visible signs of the years had dropped away. My weight had been redistributed over my body, thus giving me a twenty-five-year-old figure and a brighter personality. My old self had been inclined to be melancholy and brooding, particularly on dull winter days. All that vanished, a demonstration of the fact that your thoughts can change you. It also showed that your bodily health is closely related to your thinking."

Yvonne's friends and pupils enthusiastically testify to how well she has succeeded in transferring her knowledge—even to skeptics. Every day letters of appreciation pile high on her desk.

"I love them. They are so rewarding," says Yvonne. "But sometimes they scare me. Some people get results I never imagined and attribute powers to me that I do not possess. I am merely the instrument of Universal Mind. Always present and all-powerful, it can give you everything you desire—if you take the trouble to contact it."

One letter I picked at random was written by a woman in her mid-fifties. "It had been several weeks since I completed your course, Yvonne, and even though I showed improvement in regard to wrinkles and sagging chin while attending classes, now all the bags and wrinkles are gone as I continue breathing pink."

A former model, who had to give up her work because of increasing weight and particularly heaviness in her legs, wrote Yvonne thus: "I have to let you know what a miracle breathing turquoise has done for me. My problem of excess weight in my legs, as you know, has been completely removed in two short months by breathing turquoise, thus enabling me to be a successful swim suit model again. I'll never be able to thank you enough."

A middle-aged business woman, who was confined to her home after twisting her knee, said: "As I told you when I first wrote, I was in great pain. Having to walk with my knee bent did not look too great. I tried heat, massage, medicine, etc., but nothing helped. After breathing orange as you told me, my knee is back to normal and it only took a few evenings. I am most grateful."

Yvonne looked distressed as I read the letter. "She makes me sound as if I am a healer. I am not. I merely try to help people to help themselves to good health. I would not presume to heal or even suggest I could. Please emphasize that."

A couple who had been married for thirty years, wishing, hoping and praying for a child came to her for help. "They had gone to doctors and taken numerous treatments without results," she said. Finally, the medical men told them flatly it was too late, they were too old. They had better adopt a child. The couple mentioned how John Wayne and several other famous people had had children late in life. Why couldn't they? Neither of them had been declared sterile by the various tests, but the child just did not come.

"When they came to me," Yvonne related, "I pointed out that all I could do for them was to help them to good health if they would follow instructions. I suggested that both of them would feel better if they breathed a deep rose shade and suggested that the man visualize himself as robust and virile and deeply in love with his wife, which I could see he was. At the same time I suggested to the wife that she inbreathe pink air and mentally direct the air to her reproductive organs, at the same time visualizing and imagining how it must be to be pregnant. I also suggested she read a book giving hints on motherhood and go through the infant needs departments of the stores to get the feeling of being an expectant mother.

"I also suggested that several times a day they sit together and visualize themselves as wrapped in a cloud of rose, alternating with a shade of pink. It was all I could do. I still remember how they looked at me, tremulous but hopeful, and I knew they would try to follow the directions I had given them.

"Six months later I had a letter saying that the wife was expecting, and later came the news that she had given birth to a baby girl. These are some of the things that make my work worthwhile and fill me with pride."

I asked Yvonne to explain how breathing rose

helped the barren couple to have a child and its general relation to the restoration of sexual vitality.

"In the psychology of colors," she said, "sex is always associated with red. Red is a triumphant color. It inflames the emotions. But there is another side of sex—the spiritual. One might describe rose as being gentler and more spiritual than red. Here's a story which illustrates how it works:

"I happened to be eating lunch in a little coffee shop popular with local business people when a graying middle-aged man, whom I had known by sight for many years, came over and asked if he could sit with me. As he had never said more than a curt hello in all the fifteen years we had seen each other I was naturally intrigued to know what he wanted. After beating around the bush with conversational trivialities he came to the point. A friend had told him I had done wonders for his wife. Could I do anything to restore his vim and vigor or was my 'stuff' only for women?

"The poor fellow looked terribly embarrassed. He listened attentively as I told him he could breathe a deep shade of rose, at the same time mentally sending the air and the color to the area needing help. I told him to visualize himself as being young and virile and then release the air slowly up the spinal cord, leaving the color down there.

"He thanked me and left, having given me the impression that he would do nothing about it. A month later I met him in the street, walking tall and straight. Yes, he said, he had tried it and it had worked. His whole life had changed."

While I was writing this article Yvonne's faith in her color therapy, which she calls Youthology, was put to its severest test. While crossing the street she tripped and fell, to awaken in the hospital with one leg broken, the bone cracked in several places, and both ankles sprained with several bones misplaced by the shock of the fall.

Although in great pain, with her leg in a cast, she insisted on going home to look after her two youngest children. The doctors had told her she would be in the cast six weeks—probably more.

"That was not for me," says Yvonne. "I began to breathe orange to eliminate the pain and it worked. I did not even have to touch the painkillers and tranquilizers the doctors had given me, but I was unhappy. I had to find a color that would heal the fracture and the cracks in half the time. Even though I got out of bed the second day I was home I was not satisfied. Frankly, I began to feel blue—because I was thinking negatively.

"One morning I answered the telephone to hear a woman I knew say she had a hunch I was feeling blue and had called to cheer me up. She hoped I wasn't losing confidence in myself and Youthology, which had helped her. So what color was I breathing to knit my bones?

"I said I didn't know. What color was water, she asked. I named all the colors I had seen in water, from clear to misty white-blue, blue-green, etc. She said she thought it was usually gray, a misty blue, or green. I ought to do something with these colors, she said, and she had called just to give me that message.

"I thanked her. Frankly, I didn't feel anything but a sense of gratitude for her thinking of me. Then something seemingly miraculous happened. I got another call from a friend who is a medium. She said she had seen in a vision that I was losing my confidence in the cosmic powers. Why didn't I approach the problem of healing my leg in a practical way? What color was bone, anyway? What color would it need to restore its strength? I said that as far as I knew it was a kind of whitish gray. Fine, she said, so why didn't I take the nerve color green, add some blue, the life-force color, swathe it in mist and apply it to my leg?

"I thanked her and hung up, literally dumbfounded. The two women who had called did not know each other. Both had snatched the thought that I needed help, from the air.

"I started breathing the colors I had carefully mixed on my mental palate—dark blue with a faint tinge of green and an overlay of white mist, mentally putting my entire right leg and both feet and ankles under this healing sphere of color. From that moment my life changed. No more negative thinking! Just happy, confidence. I felt lighter on my feet and in spirit.

"On my next hospital visit the doctor said, 'You really must live right. You're almost ready to come out of the cast. I can't believe it, but there it is.' I didn't dare tell him I had been using my own color therapy.

"A week later I shed my cast and went home elated until I noticed that my leg looked terrible, shapeless and discolored. The message came clearly: I was to have faith and keep breathing. I did. Now the leg looks as good as the other . . . and I've always had nice legs."

I asked Yvonne what color one should breathe to attract others—interesting and/or lonely people.

"You just breathe a nice bright green and see them swathed in it. They'll come running. Hold the picture in your imagination and you'll be surprised at the result. It works whether you want to attract the person for business or romance or just friendship. Try it, but remember, you must use your imagination."

Yvonne smiled. "It works with me. I've just married again—a darling man."

COMMENTS ON THE ABOVE ARTICLE

Yvonne is her own best example of her method. I have a recent, colored, unretouched picture of her taken on Mother's Day, 1974, in a Chicago Hotel dining room. She truly appears amazing. She is not only beautiful, but although she is reaching fifty—a grandmother and a new mother of a four-year-old—she looks as if she were in her thirties or even younger. She says her former wrinkles and bags under her eyes have disappeared, which the photograph confirms.

Although I have not met her, I wrote to her asking questions about her method so that we can all understand it better. She is writing a book about it in greater detail, but meanwhile here are her answers, which throw more light on the technique:

Q. What shade of pink do you use?

A. A light warm "baby" pink, containing a touch of lavender. [She sent me a sample.]

Q. How do you do the actual breathing?

A. First, I take several deep breaths (this could be of pink air). Then I choose one area at a time to work on. For example, I had a wrinkle on one cheek. I spread it smooth with my fingers so I could see how that area would look with the wrinkle removed. To treat that area with color breathing, I first breathed in pink air, then, *while I held my breath,* I visualized the skin area as smooth and unwrinkled. Next I exhaled slowly. I repeated this breath plus visualization two more times, making three total breaths for that area. After working on one area, I proceed to another.

I do the whole process first thing upon awakening and the last thing at night before going to sleep. If I can get away by myself during the day, I repeat it. You can do it anywhere—even while driving.

Q. How long does it take for results?

A. It took me eight months. It has taken others from months to years. After a while, every day I became aware that I was being made over by the pink color I breathed. Eventually I not only woke up feeling better, but I began looking better. The wrinkles and bags I had acquired during my thirties were going! My vitality increased and my physical health improved steadily. The change was as visible to others as it was to me. A doctor who later checked me said, "You have the body of a woman half your age. I really can't believe it."

Q. Have others been able to accomplish the same results you have experienced?

A. Yes. I have many letters in my files as well as before-and-after pictures of satisfied users, both men and women. One woman wrote me, "I still cannot believe what has happened to me. Halfway through your lessons I began to change all over. Before that I was a pill popper, using pills for everything. But one morning after beginning your program, I awoke feeling glad to be alive for the first time in years. I settled down to my color breathing in earnest and in time looked as I had ten years earlier before bags, wrinkles and worry lines had taken over. I haven't taken a pill since. I don't need them anymore. I also lost excess pounds as well as aches and pains."

Although the color pink is used for rejuvenation, Yvonne also used other colors for healing purposes. She chooses the color to fit the condition (as I have described in the separate colors earlier) and then couples it with breathing. She visualizes it as being directed to the part of the body needing help. She explains that this is not magic; it is merely the life force at work: the vibration of the color is used to raise the vibration of that part of the body. Actually, it is akin to biofeedback, a form of mind control, initiated by the Elmer

Greens and their associates at the Menninger Clinic. Blood pressure, pulse rates, and body heat have been brought under control by this method, as proved by a biofeedback machine which registers the change.

Until Yvonne's book is available, as a result of my own experience and that of others I know who are trying this color breathing, the following tips may help make it easier for you. Otherwise some people may prematurely give in to discouragement because it may not be as easy for them as for others. Those who are already disciplined in yoga breathing seem to find it easier to do.

Color breathing requires deep concentration. Often your mind tends to wander, or you "lose" your color of pink in your mind. If it is at bedtime, you may fall asleep before you finish.

SUGGESTIONS FOR THE READER

1. Colors are hard for some people to remember. It is not only a problem of choosing the shade of pink, but of being able to hang on to it mentally. Some people feel more attracted to one shade of pink than another, and conseq ntly may recall it more easily. Some esoteric writers, as I will clarify later, advocate a rosy pink as being effective.

So choose a shade of pink which attracts *you*. I found that pink geraniums in my garden were close to Yvonne's pink, but I liked the pink of a cyclamen growing nearby even better, so I often use that shade.

You may stop at a paint store and get a color card of various pinks from which to choose, or find an appropriate pink swatch of fabric, a scarf, or a picture. Whatever you choose, keep it near you while meditating in order to refresh your memory vividly as needed.

2. As you visualize it, you may picture the pink color coming from the atmosphere directly into your nostrils. Or you may first surround yourself with a pink cloud or aura and breathe in from that, or just breathe in pink air.

3. After having decided what shade of pink to use and how to inhale it, you will need to have your new body blueprint (perhaps we should call it a pink-print) all ready to visualize in order to get the desired results before your mind's eye. Decide what you wish to improve. If it is hard for you to visualize, use the most attractive picture of yourself at an earlier age you can find, as a guide. If it doesn't suit you, make necessary changes in your mind. Perhaps you now want a better figure than you once had, or a thicker head of hair, or whatever. Incorporate these corrections into your new mental picture of yourself and have it ready to use, area by area.

You could start by filling your lungs fully with pink air, then say, silently or aloud, "I wish to have a perfect figure." Breathe in pink air, and, *on the holding breath*, bathe the area you are working on in pink, then visualize your new picture, as you planned it. Repeat twice more. Then proceed to another area. By having all the "props" ready, you will find it easier to concentrate. Also do not vary your picture until it has been acquired. Once you have decided upon the improvement you desire, stick to it for best results. Changing your mind or your picture daily could dilute progress.

4. If you are breathing color for health, here is a method suggested by S.G.J. Ouseley in his book on color therapy.* He says, "Close your eyes and when you have mentally contemplated the desired color three minutes, expel all the air from your lungs and stomach and relax all of your muscles until your body is as limp as possible.

"Then inhale the colored breath deeply, carrying it to your ribs and chest. As you breathe in the color, count up to eight, Hold your breath for eight seconds and last, exhale for eight counts."

Other writers explain, "Once inhaled, the 'colored breath' is directed to and focused on the seat of affliction, if any. It is during the *holding* breath that you visualize the desired condition, holding your breath only as long as comfortable."

Ouseley adds, "It is also important to feel conscious of, and visualize, the inflow of color revitalizing and replenishing the entire system."

Yvonne has admitted that not only her appearance has been rejuvenated by inhaling pink air every day, but she has had a complete change of personality as well. She has become a more loving, radiant, happy person, she says. This may be explained by the Rosicrucian concept of the color pink. This is a rosy pink which the Rosicrucians consider the color of universal love, and they believe that by visualizing this color for yourself and others, universal love will become manifest in the body, mind and emotions. Since love represents the greatest constructive vibration in the universe, it is not surprising that applied regularly, as in

* S. G. J. Ouseley: *The Power of the Rays—The Science of Color Healing*. L. W. Fowler & Co., Stuart House, 1 Tudor Street, London E.C. 4, England

breathing in pink, your whole being could change for the better.*

Yvonne sums up, "Once you begin to learn and work with this concept of color breathing, you *will* begin to change for the better. You will also wonder how you ever lived without it."

Several of my friends and I have just begun to use this technique. Since we are beginners, it is too early to expect or report results. But we have developed a fun slogan to remind each other to keep at it. At the end of a conversation, a phone call or a letter, we always conclude with the sign of: THINK PINK!

---

* Joseph J. Weed: *Wisdom of the Mystic Masters.* Pp. 124–125, paper edition, eighth printing, 1970. Parker Publishing Company, West Nyack, New York

Bibliography

COLOR THERAPY

Alder, Vera Stanley. *The Finding of the Third Eye*, Samuel Weiser, Inc., New York. Third impression, 1972
  The Secret of the Atomic Age, Samuel Weiser, Inc., New York, 1972

Amber, R. B. *Color Therapy*, Firma K. L. Mukhopadhyay, Calcutta, 1964

Babbitt, Edwin D., M.D. *The Principles of Light and Color*, Spectrochrome Institute, Malaga, N. J., 1925. Originally published by the author (Babbitt & Co.), New York, 1878

Birren, Faber. *Color Psychology and Color Therapy*, University Books, Inc., New Hyde Park, N. Y., 1961

Brunler, Oscar, M.D. *Rays and Radiation Phenomena*, De Vorss & Co., Los Angeles, 1948
———. *Astrophysics*, London, 1937

Burroughs, Stanley A. *Living Creatively Through Vita-Flex, Color Vibration and Nutrition*, self-published. (No date)

Clark, Linda. *Are You Radioactive? How to Protect Yourself*, The Devin-Adair Co., Old Greenwich, Conn. 06870, 1973
———. *Get Well Naturally*, The Devin-Adair Co., Old Greenwich, Conn. 06870. Second editon, 1974

Color Digest. Higgins Ink Co., Brooklyn, N.Y., 1953

Color Dynamics for the Home. Pittsburgh Plate Glass Co., Tampa, Fla. (No date)

Color Healing. An Exhaustive Survey Compiled from 21 Works of the Leading Practitioners of Chromotherapy, Health Research, Mokelumne Hill, Cal., 1956

Colton, Anne Ree. *Ethical ESP*, ARC Publishing Co., P.O. Box 1138, Glendale, Calif. 91209, 1971

———. *Watch Your Dreams.* ARC Publishing Co., P.O. Box 1138, Glendale, Cal. 91209, 1973

Day, Langston and De La Warr, George. *New Worlds Beyond the Atom*, The Devin-Adair Co., Old Greenwich, Conn. 06870, 1959

Ellinger, Friedrich. *The Biologic Fundamentals of Radiation Therapy*, Elsevier Publishing Co., Inc., New York, 1961

Fielding, William J. *The Marvels and Oddities of Sunlight*, Little Blue Book No. 1563, Haldeman-Julius Publications, Girard, Kansas. (No date)

Finch, Elizabeth and W. J. *Photo-Chromotherapy*, Esoteric Publications, P.O. Box 11288, Phoenix, Arizona 85017. (No date)

Ghadiali, Col. Dinshah P., M.Sc. *Spectro-Chrome-Metry Encyclopedia*, Volumes I, II, III, Spectro-Chrome Institute, Malaga, N. J., 1939

Goethe's Theory of Color. Applied by Maria Schindler, New Knowledge Books, Sussex, England, 1964

Griffiths, Joel, and Ballantine, Richard. *Silent Slaughter*, Henry Regnery Co., Chicago, 1972

Hanoka, N.S., N.D., D.D.S. *The Advantages of Healing by Visible Spectrum Therapy*, Bharti Association Publications, Ghaziabad, U.P., India, 1957

Heline, Corinne. *Healing and Regeneration Through Color.* J. F. Rownery Press, Santa Barbara, Cal. Tenth edition, 1964

Hetherington, Rex D. *Color—Its Power Action and Therapeutic Value.* (No publishing data available)

Howat, R. Douglas. *Elements of Chromotherapy*, Actinic Press, London, 1938

Hunt, Roland T. *Complete Color Prescription*, De Vorss & Co., Los Angeles, 1962

Kargere, Audrey, Ph.D. *Color and Personality*, Occult Research Press, 117 Fourth Ave., New York 10003, or Wehman Bros., Publishers, 712 Broadway, New York 10003

Leadbetter, C. W. *Man Visible and Invisible*, Theosophical Publishing Society, London, 1971

Lewis, Roger. *Color and the Edgar Cayce Readings*, A.R.E. Press, Virginia Beach, Va. 25450, 1973

Luckiesh, M. *Ultra Violet Radiation*, D. Van Nostrand Co., New York, 1922

Luckiesh, M., and Pacini, A. J. *Light and Health*, The Williams & Wilkins Co., Baltimore, Md., 1926

Mayer, Gladys. *Colour and Healing*, Health Research, Mokelumne Hill, Cal., 1963

Natural Method of Healing Cataract. Book #186, Vestpocket Natural Health Library, Benedict Lust Publications, New York, 1961

Ostrander, Sheila, and Schroeder, Lynn. *Psychic Discoveries Behind the Iron Curtain*, Bantam Books, New York. Sixth printing, 1971

Ott, John N. *Health & Light: The Effects of Natural and Artificial Light on Man and Other Living Things*, The Devin-Adair Co., Old Greenwich, Conn. 06870, 1973

———. *My Ivory Cellar*, The Devin-Adair Co., Old Greenwich, Conn. 06870, 1971. Originally published by the author (John Ott Pictures, Inc.), Chicago, 1958

Ouseley, S. G. J. *The Power of the Rays*, L. N. Fowler Co. Ltd., London. Fourth edition, 1963

Pancoast, S. *Blue and Red Light*, J. M. Stoddart & Co., Philadelphia, 1877

Podolsky, Edward, M.D. *How to Charm with Color*, Herald Publishing Co., (No date)

Sander, C. G. *Color in Health and Disease*, The C. W. Daniel Co., London. Seventh edition. (No date)

———. *The Seven Keys of Color Healing*, The C. W. Daniel Co., London. Seventh edition. (No date)

Scott, Ian. *The Lüscher Color Test* (based on the

original German text by Dr. Max Lüscher), Pocket Books, New York, 1971

Simpkins, R. Brooks. *Visible Ray Therapy of the Eyes*, Health Science Press, Rustington, Sussex, England, 1963

Snow, William Benham, M.D. *The Therapeutics of Radiant Light and Heat and Convective Heat*, Scientific Authors Publishing Co., New York, 1909

Stevens, Ernest J., M.Sc., Ph.D. *Lights, Colors, Tones and Nature's Finer Forces*, self-published by E. J. Stevens Research Laboratories, San Francisco, 1923

Tompkins, Peter, and Bird, Christopher. *The Secret Life of Plants*, Harper & Row, New York, 1973

Winslow, Dr. Forbes. *The Influence of Life and Health*. (No publishing data available)

GEM THERAPY

Bhattacharyya, Benoytosh, Ph.D. *VIBGYOR, The Science of Cosmic Ray Therapy*, Good Companions Publishers, Baroda, India, 1957

Fernie, W. T., M.D. *Precious Stones (Curative)*, John Wright & Co., Bristol, England, 1907

Gems and Stones. A comprehensive study based upon the Edgar Cayce Readings, A.R.E. Press, Virginia Beach, Va. 23450, 1960, 1964

MacDonald, Howard Brenton, M.D., F.R.C.S. *Esmeralda, The Healing Properties of Gems, Jewels and Metals*. (Published in England; out of print.)

Tansley, David V., D.C. *Radionics and the Subtle Anatomy of Man*, Health Science Press, Rustington, Sussex, England, 1972

AURAS

Besant, Annie, and Leadbetter, C. W. *Thought Forms*. Contains 58 color and black and white illustrations; a Quest Book, The Theosophical Publishing House, Wheaton, Ill. Ninth edition, 1972

Bhattacharyya, Benoytosh, Ph.D. *VIBGYOR, The Sci-*

ence of Cosmic Ray Therapy, Good Companions Publishers, Baroda, India, 1957

Cayce, Edgar. *Auras,* A.R.E. Publishing Co., Virginia Beach, Va. 23450

Clark, Linda. *Help Yourself to Health,* Pyramid Publications, New York, 1972

————. *Stay Young Longer,* The Devin-Adair Co., Old Greenwich, 1961; Pyramid Publications, 1968

Leadbetter, C. W. *Man Visible and Invisible.* Contains 22 colored illustrations; a Quest Book, The Theosophical Publishing House, Wheaton, Ill. Eighth edition, 1971

Ouseley, S. G. J. *The Science of the Aura,* L. N. Fowler Ltd., 15 New Bridge Street, London, E.C.4. Seventh printing, 1968

Thedick, Eleanore. *The Bridge of Color.*

————. *Jewels of Truth and Rays of Color.* Both titles available from The Christ Ministry Foundation, 2100 Bowling Green Drive, Sacramento, Cal. 95825

Weed, Joseph J. *Wisdom of the Mystic Masters.* Parker Publishing Co., W. Nyack, N.Y. Eighth printing, 1970

HEALTHY IS BEAUTIFUL

Shape Up Within & Without

Whatever your interests, whatever your needs, Pocket Books has the best books to help you look good and feel good.

_____ 82382	**BACKACHE: STRESS & TENSION** H. Kraus, M.D.	$2.25
_____ 42239	**BODYBUILDING FOR EVERYONE** Lou Ravelle	$2.25
_____ 41445	**CARLTON FREDERICK'S CALORIE & CARBOHYDRATE GUIDE** Carlton Fredericks	$2.50
_____ 41646	**COMPLETE ILLUSTRATED BOOK OF YOGA** Swami Vishnudevananda	$2.95
_____ 41759	**CONSUMER GUIDE TO A FLATTER STOMACH**	$2.50
_____ 83406	**DICTIONARY OF NUTRITION** Richard Ashley & Heidi Duggal	$2.50
_____ 41651	**FAMILY MEDICAL ENCYCLOPEDIA** J. Schifferes, Ph.D.	$3.50
_____ 82608	**FEEL LIKE A MILLION** Elwood	$2.50
_____ 83236	**HEALTH & LIGHT** John Ott	$2.25
_____ 41053	**HOW TO STOP SMOKING** Herbert Brean	$2.50
_____ 41763	**JOY OF RUNNING** Thaddeus Kostrubala	$2.25
_____ 41768	**TOTAL FITNESS IN 30 MINUTES A WEEK** Laurence E. Morehouse, Ph.D.	$2.50